The Death of Liberty & Democracy:

The Conservative War on America & the Growth of American Fascism

CHARLES MALONE

ISBN: 0988333821
ISBN-13: 978-0-9883338-2-6

To My wife and wonderful children.

CONTENTS

Chapter 1: Introduction   1

Chapter 2: An American Theocracy: Revolt Against Our Plural   57
Liberal Democratic Republic

Chapter 3: Conservatives & The Death of American Civil   84
Liberties

Chapter 4: U.S. Conservative Foreign Policy: From Isolation to   122
World Domination

Chapter 5: Conservatism & White Supremacy: Two Peas in a   164
Pod

Chapter 6: Independent Judiciary: The Attack on the Last   201
Defender of Liberty

Chapter 7: Changing Our Future   223

Bibliography   257

ACKNOWLEDGMENTS

For all those Americans out there working to expose the corruption, bias, and favoritism within the American government through their podcasts, books, websites, radio shows, and other means, I thank you. It is you have inspired me to do my part to return control of the government to its rightful possessors, the American people.

CHAPTER 1: INTRODUCTION

In the aftermath of Hurricane Katrina, Americans learned that the conservatives leading the legislative and executive branches of the United States Government loathed the working class and the poor in America. They ignored New Orleans and the Gulf Coast despite the destruction, the lack of safe drinking water, and the toxic sludge. They turned a blind eye as multibillion dollar insurance companies denied legitimate claims on the basis that it was water (excluded from coverage) that damaged the home despite the fact that the water entered most of the homes because it was blown in by the wind (covered by most insurance policies). These events still did not serve as a wakeup call for most Americans that the conservatives in power cared more about the wealthy elite and corporate interests because the "liberal media" portrayed it as if it were only a problem for Black New Orleanians despite tens of thousands of poor white southerners being in dire situations as well. In fact, the "liberal media" had its opportunity to report the true suffering and class disparities exhibited by the government's lack of response to the Katrina event but decided to report stories meant to portray African Americans as looting for food and water and white Americans finding food and water, further reinforcing white stereotypes of African Americans.

What is crystal clear in the aftermath of Katrina is that instead of serving the people, as government is intended, the conservative-led government serves corporate America. As will be demonstrated throughout this book, destruction of a people's liberty demoralizes them and makes them afraid for their future and anxious to protect the little they have. However, the ultimate effect of destroying the people's liberty is that the people are so afraid and/or demoralized that they are unwilling to standup and fight for themselves making that much easier for government to focus on protecting corporate assets and profits.

1

The conservative government was so out of touch with working class and poor Americans that conservative President George W. Bush did not set foot in New Orleans during the first 72 hours after the flooding began instead focusing on completing his vacation as opposed to showing the people of the Gulf Coast he cared. Kanye West had it half right when he said that George Bush does not care about Black people because the truth is George Bush, like most silver spoon rich boys, does not care about working class people. A major American city and dozens of other American towns and cities were inundated by a natural disaster and faulty levees but the President of the United States did not give the affected Americans the time of day.

Even more telling were President Bush's mother's racist and immoral comments about the poor people living in the Astrodome being better off than they were before the flooding despite the fact that many of the people had lost loved ones in the flooding and all of their worldly possessions. This should have been America's Marie Antoinette moment because it showed exactly uncaring America's aristocracy truly is but the demoralized and scared public only worried about losing their individual crumbs thrown to them by the wealthy elite not realizing that there are powers in numbers.

These facts illustrate the general approach of American conservatives toward the average American. If you are not a corporate elite or a member of the American aristocracy (i.e. a Bush), the conservative philosophy of government is that you do not count. Out of this approach to governance arises many concerns about the future of America under the leadership of the homogenous conservative Republican Party. For example, how did America get to this point? Where are we headed as a country? Are we going to continue to allow the pseudo-religious conservatives' attempt to pacify the mass of the working class and middle class by incessantly distracting them with ridiculous issues such as flag burning, prayer in public schools, and anti-homosexual messages? Or will we begin the long arduous task of giving America back to its citizens? Will we demand more from our government in the form of public services for our tax money rather than corporate welfare continuing? These questions are central to any liberal/progressive revival in America.

Currently, the United States is under the control of conservatives and it has been since the early post-colonial days of the republic despite a few true liberal exceptions to the rule like the New Deal Era and the Civil Rights Movement power shifted from the corporate board rooms to the common man. In both of these instances, the people demanded that government work for them and not Wall Street resulting in expanded liberty with the long-term effects of creating the middle class, as happened as a result of the New Deal programs, and expansion of the middle class by allowing people of color, a direct result of the Civil Rights movement, the same opportunities afforded to white Americans. This illustrates that liberty is not just about individuals being free from government control but it is also about the people controlling government. The key to any long-term revival of liberty for the people is through the Constitution.

Despite their claims of supporting the Constitution, conservatives in America have historically done the opposite. While our Constitution stands for liberty for the people, conservatives have promoted an ideology of order with an eye toward protecting the status quo even when that status quo clearly violated the Constitution as was the case with the adoption and continuation of Jim Crow segregation after the Fourteenth Amendment's ratification, promoting violent attacks against labor organizers through the use of hired thugs early in the Industrial Revolution, and enabling corporations to control the American political landscape with their money rather than the people with their voices. When liberals and progressives begin to challenge the long held power of conservatives, they responded with violent confrontations and efforts to control the media and reduce to bare bones the public education system and our universities; the institutions that should provide the people with the knowledge necessary to challenge the status quo, respectively.

As will be shown later, if America were truly built on those fundamental principles enshrined in our Constitution, conservatism would probably not be able to survive in America. However, the attack on America's fundamental principles was accomplished with a smile of sincerity as conservative leaders told the American public that their actions were in the interest of promoting personal responsibility, advancing liberty, upholding the Constitution, and restoring America to its mythical past of being a Christian nation.[1] In reality, the conservatives' policies promoted the interests of the plutocracy by protecting the status quo through propaganda and subterfuge. The status quo consists of the concentration of the wealth of the nation in the hands of the few, low voter turnout as working class and poor Americans become disenchanted with the system and refuse to participate, increasing numbers of people qualified only for low wage and unskilled service industry jobs because of a combination of the antiquated educational system and skilled jobs moving offshore,

---

[1] I find this last idea the most fanciful and ridiculous when one considers that during much of America's history the so-called Christian majority lynched, raped, and enslaved African Americans in the name of God. The lynchings were perhaps the most brutal events because soon after attending their religious services, white Americans in the South and Midwest would attend evening lynchings where some poor soul would have his genitalia, fingers, and hands cutoff and his body burned for the simple allegation of looking at a white woman or some other criminal violation like being uppity.

millions of American families are mired in debt with very little in savings because our economy is propped up on the notion that Americans should spend every dime they have turning many into wage slaves who do not have the option of following their dreams, and astronomical prison populations where many offenders should be in mental health or chemical dependency treatment facilities rather than prison just to name a few of the problems created by conservatives view of the world. Conservatives want to protect this status quo because it ensures that the masses will be ill-equipped to challenge the American plutocracy's hegemony.

The propaganda and subterfuge used by conservatives since the founding of America has consisted of the systematic rewriting of contemporary and historical facts about America to mislead the people. For example, conservatives often claim that America's health care system is the best in the world but when one looks at infant mortality and life expectancy as compared to other developed/industrialized nations (i.e. EU, Japan, Canada), America's is the worst but the coverage by our "liberal media" would never disclose those facts to the public at large nor would it disclose the number of bankruptcies Americans file related to medical bills. Instead, the "liberal media" focuses on how wonderful the technology is that the United States' medical community utilizes to diagnose patients with nary a mention that nearly 100 million Americans are uninsurable because of preexisting conditions, cannot afford medical insurance premiums, or are underinsured because their employers can only afford stripped down insurance policies that do not really provide the needed medical services preventing them from enjoying the benefits of this wonderful technology. Additionally, Americans never learn that their medical insurance has a maximum lifetime dollar value for coverage unless they suffer some catastrophic illness or injury.

By misleading the people, conservatives are able to prevent any popular reforms to a broken system thus protecting their status quo; increasing profits for their friends like the corporate health insurance providers. Since conservatives took over Congress in 1994 and declared a "Contract with America"[2] under the auspices of infamous then-House Speaker Newt Gingrich, they have dragged America away from her core principles into an abyss of authoritarianism and proto-fascist policies in an effort to stave off the political left's attempts to bring the people up to speed about the dire circumstances that face America environmentally, politically, socially, economically, and culturally as well as begin addressing these issues with new public policy solutions that are not profit-centered

---

[2] Some would say a "Contract On America." I first heard this term from a good friend of mine from law school named Brett Mangum who is currently practicing law in Kentucky.

but human-centered as government should. The vision that conservatives have of America is substantially different from that held by the liberals responsible for drafting our Constitution and its companion Bill of Rights.

The men who attended the Philadelphia Constitutional Convention during that long, hot summer of 1787 behind closed doors decided that the nation-state that they would create needed to be different from the world as they knew it. These men wanted America to be a forward looking nation; a nation that had abandoned the largely sectarian strife rampant in Old Europe. They knew that in order to do that they would need to entrench in our fundamental law, the Constitution, some new principles about the proper role of government in society. Many of the principles were borrowed from classical liberal philosophers John Locke, John Stuart Mills, and others. It would be these very principles that would ensure the people's liberty.

Out of classical liberalism arose four fundamental principles upon which America would stand; the Founding Fathers wanted America to be a **PLURAL LIBERAL DEMOCRATIC REPUBLIC**. The new country would be **plural** in that people of all ideologies, faiths, persuasions, beliefs, and principles would be welcomed to openly express their opinions without regard to whether those opinions were consistent with the majority of society's opinions or the government's viewpoint. This included preventing the government imposition of, or financial support for, one religious faith as in England where the Church of England was the state church supported by taxpayer funds. America would be **liberal** in that all individuals would be free to determine what to do with their lives, how to live their lives, and free to pursue their passions without undue governmental interference. Individuals should decide who they marry, whether they want to have children, how to raise those children, where they wish to reside, whether they wish to participate in any religious ceremonies or events, and many other activities that free persons have a right to decide.[3] The United States would be **democratic** because the government would govern with the consent of the people and when that consent is withdrawn the government ceases to have authority. In the eighteenth century, the kings of Europe claimed a right to rule as a matter of birth, which meant that the people often played little or no role in the selection of their governments. In America, that would all change because the people would be directly and

---

[3] This is really at the center of substantive due process rights that are under attack from conservatives like Associate Justice Antonin Scalia because he says they are a sham in that there is no support for substantive due process in the Constitution. However, the Founding Fathers made clear in drafting and ratifying our basic law that the Constitution is a limited Constitution. With that being said, where power is not in the hands of the federal government it remains in the hands of the sovereign people.

indirectly responsible for selecting their leaders. Lastly, America would be a **republic** because the Founding Fathers believed that sovereignty should flow directly from the people not some individual claiming a divine right to rule from God. While this is similar to the democracy principle, it differs in that the people ultimately determine the type of government they have and how much or how little authority that government has, in a republic. The people's sovereign authority gives them the power to abolish a dissatisfactory system of government as was the case when the Articles of Confederation were replaced as an unworkable system of government. These four fundamental principles, which are the foundation upon which American society stands, may seem simple but they were, and remain so today, far-reaching concepts that attempt to take governing authority out of the hands of the few and place it in the hands of the many by making society open to a discussion of broad ideas and open so that any person may pursue his or her desires.

The Founding Fathers drafted the U.S. Constitution to embody these principles with the intent of having a Constitution that was not a meaningless political document as was the case throughout Europe at the time but one that was a legal document, which was a precedent setting approach to government. As a legal document embodying our four fundamental principles, it would place limitations on government power. These constitutional limitations represent what is known as the Rule of Law as government would no longer be able to act arbitrarily and unconstrained toward the people. We will return to a discussion of the Rule of Law concept later. The main point is that these four fundamental principles were contrary to much of the world as it existed for the Founding Fathers as differences of political and/or religious opinion were abhorred and criminally punished and, sometimes, resulted in civil warfare. European societies' main institutions were very conservative in promoting the status quo and attacking individual liberty, monarchs were often despotic autocrats who did not answer to the people. As will be shown throughout this book, the modern American conservative's viewpoint is often aligned with these old, outdated European ways as they attempt to protect the corporate elite and the concentration of wealth in the hands of the few just as the Old Order was protected in seventeenth and eighteenth century Europe.

Central to the dogma of classical conservatism is this idea that the status quo should be preserved; that is to say society's traditions should not come under critical scrutiny. For the conservative, traditions preserved order in society; conservatives saw individual liberty as something that led to chaos in society as individuals as well as the masses could not be trusted to govern themselves so society needed to limit its citizens' ability to make decisions for themselves through various institutions that include, but are not limited to, the law, religion, and social mores. Order takes on more importance than liberty in conservative ideology because it is really intended to protect the propertied elite and the wealth of the aristocracy. It instills in citizens fear and docility, which inhibits their willingness to challenge the establishment for fear of losing what little they have as well as passivity and docility as society's major institutions, established law, ideologies, and leaders are not questioned because they know what is right for you. Instead of the people doing things because they make sense and are consistent with their happiness as the fundamental right of liberty would have it, conservatives want people to do things because it has always been that way and it protects the interests of the elites. This lunacy is alive and well in the American conservative movement.

The rise of classical conservatism can be traced to the developments of the Age of Enlightenment and the Age of Reason. These two important periods in human history challenged the status quo in a major way. These ages led to great advances in government, economics, physics, chemistry, and biology as a result of great thinkers' critically analyzing the established doctrines and institutions. While our Founding Fathers were greatly influenced by the Enlightenment as shown in the drafting of the Constitution and despite the advancements of the Enlightenment provided, conservatives responded to the Enlightenment by proclaiming that traditions should be preserved for the sake of tradition. In fact, the father of classical conservatism, Edmund Burke, wildly opposed to the principle of liberty that arose from the Enlightenment and advanced by the French Revolution. Burke, as conservatives continue to believe today, advanced the idea that society cannot survive without tradition and predicted that France would never survive as an ordered society because the tried and true traditions were disposed of en masse. Of course, we know that Burke and other conservatives of his era were completely wrong because France is a modern industrial power with one of the best standards of living in the world despite the disposition of the aristocratic and monarchical traditions.

The French Revolution focused on liberty for all men and sought to destroy those institutions that prevented the attainment of that liberty. In throwing off the shackles of monarchy and aristocracy in France, the slogan became "Liberty, Equality, and Fraternity," which remains the motto of republican France to this day. Yes, French revolutionaries killed thousands of aristocrats, monarchists, and their sympathizers. However, conservatives failed to recognize the real causes of the so-called Reign of Terror in France. It was not simply blood thirsty mobs of Frenchmen killing for the sake of killing. The cause was a failure by the French aristocracy to loosen the reins on the people economically, politically, and socially. Government did not respond to the needs and desires of the people; it only advanced the interests of the few over those of the many. That failure ultimately led to the dispatching of the aristocracy by guillotine as they were directly responsible for imposing the feudal system on the French people that stood in the way of true liberty in France.

With its roots tainted by the stench of an anti-liberty message, no wonder the modern American conservative is predisposed to using the people's government and media against them to prevent the advancing the people's interests. It is not a "Reign of Terror" when the masses throw off the chains of oppression girded to their backs by the uncompassionate elite. Just as pre-revolutionary France's government embodied all the things wrong with aristocracy and plutocracy so to does modern America's conservatives who control our government and "liberal media." However, the modern American conservative is even more dangerous than Burke and his ilk who opposed the French Revolution despite pre-revolutionary France not having any constitutional guarantees protecting the people from arbitrary governance. American conservatives have declared war on the U.S. Constitution and the limitations it places on government power. American conservatives use propaganda to convince Americans that useless traditions are worth protecting and continuing while simultaneously successfully indoctrinating Americans in the belief that their Constitution is filled with technicalities where individual rights are concerned or does not really mean what it says in the case of religious establishment.

Modern American conservatives, for example, have successfully convinced huge swaths of the American population that evolution is evil and a fiction because it supposedly goes against all the teachings of Christianity about how the human race arose on the earth despite the sound science of carbon dating and the fossil record behind the concept of evolution. Just as the Christian church had it wrong about the sun revolving around earth or about the world being flat, it continues to be wrong about this particular matter of scientific fact and that is why religion should stay out of matters of science and focus on matters of spirituality as it is intended. This is just one example of American conservatives using a long antiquated tradition to prevent progress and the advancement of the people's knowledge and understanding of the world because that advancement does not fit well within the conservative's social construct for controlling the people. It is this advancement and many others that lead conservatives to reminisce for a past when traditions were held.

Oftentimes, this reminiscing takes on a reactionary approach in the face of some of these controversial advancements (i.e. abortion, physician assisted suicide, gay and lesbian equality, and repealing the death penalty). In opposition to individual liberty, which is directly advanced by many of these controversial issues, conservatives form groups like Focus on the Family and the Family Research Council out of fear of what they cannot control so they want to use the power of the government to control it for them; they fear that many Americans do want to decide whether they should carry the pregnancy through to its full-term or whether to terminate it for other personal reasons, they fear that many Americans might become accepting of homosexual relationships as normal in society as schools attempt to teach children acceptance of people as they are, and the fear that many Americans, when faced with excruciating pain related to some terminal illness, may decide to take their own life with the assistance of lethal drugs prescribed by a physician. Despite their claims of supporting liberty conservatives are clearly anti-liberty because these positions are at the core of what government should not be involved in. Faced with an uphill battle in persuading Americans that these things encompass too much liberty, some of the conservatives' messages have taken on the sinister characteristics of the fascist regimes of the early twentieth century.

Conservatives respond to this factual representation with self-righteous indignation and anger after having already pejoratively called their political opponents "liberal," "Communists," or "socialists." Conservatives engage in name calling as a way to deflect attention from their own shortcomings; the modern conservative is wise enough to know that acknowledging that their policies and plans are inconsistent with America's fundamental principles would spell the death of the conservative movement as Americans are well aware of the oppressive nature of fascist regimes of the past as were exhibited in Hitler's concentration camps. At its core, fascism is an extreme reactionary, right-wing political ideology in which a single political party led by a dictator who, using the authority of the state, dominates all aspects of society by using law enforcement, the media, and the armed forces to crush internal dissent.[4] Supreme within a fascist-dominated society are the leader, the party, and the state respectively; that is to say that "the interest of the state always [take] precedence over the right of the individual."[5] The guiding principles of fascism are:

---

[4] Many people wrongly think that German Nazis were socialist because their party's name was Nationalist Socialist German Workers Party but they were actually vehemently opposed to socialist, Marxist, and liberal democracy.

[5] Walter Laqueur, *Fascism: Past, Present, Future*, (New York: Oxford University Press, Inc., 1996), 25.

Nationalism: extreme patriotism; a belief that one's national culture is superior to all others and that anything different is a threat	Militarism: the state pursues its domestic and international goals through armed force; security can only exist through the use of military force; going on the offensive (preemptive war)
Racism: the state and its officials take the position that some groups of people are naturally inferior to other groups of people, as such there is no need for equality, which also justifies the subjugation of those inferior people	Imperialism: the state extends control over foreign states for racial, economic, and/or political reasons; it can be done directly through military occupation or indirectly through foreign policy/economic practices
State domination of Religion: religious organizations are dominated by the state. They receive funding from the state and their very existence is dependent upon the state's consent; there is no free exercise of religion or belief because religion is used as a way reinforce the regime's policies	Corporatism: Big business enters into a parasitic relationship with the government where corporations provide money and material to the ruling party in exchange for preferential treatment in receiving contracts and monopolies over certain industries; big business enterprises that provide the necessary money and material are largely left alone to continue to operate as they see fit

These fascist principles are completely contrary to America's Constitution. Nevertheless, elements of these principles can be found throughout the American conservative movement historically and contemporarily. For the fascists to successfully implement their core principles, fascists need to engage in the extensive use of propaganda. Along with the need for a strong propaganda machine, fascists also use violence and intimidation to attack those who do not support their message. Benito Mussolini pioneered these tactics in Italy. In Nazi Germany, Adolf Hitler co-opted much of Mussolini's tactics and in fact refined them. Hitler employed one of the most effective uses of the propaganda machine, led by propaganda minister Joseph Paul Goebbels, to dupe the German people into believing his talk of returning Germany to its mythical former glory and explaining how the German nation was being held back by inferior people like the Jews, Roma, and disabled who were taking advantage of the Aryan people.

Hitler's theory on the use of propaganda consisted of "making a few points for mass consumption and then endlessly repeating them."[6] Hitler believed that most people could be swayed through messages that reached out to their raw emotions because most people were unintelligent and unwilling to search out the truth. In fact Hitler was partially right as many Germans were swayed by these misleading messages. When propaganda was not sufficient, Hitler resorted to the use of force to suppress dissent among the German people using organizations like the Gestapo (secret police responsible for internal security), led by Heinrich Himmler, and the Schutzstaffel (SS), which was an elite military/police unit within the Nazi Party.

The American conservative movement has employed many of the same tactics as the fascists in Hitler's Germany. In the first half of the twentieth century, Americans were taught to fear the stalking Communists, which led to a demonization so great that many Americans believed Communists would sneak into their homes and murder them in their sleep. With the fall of the Iron Curtain one would think that the demonization would come to an end. However, conservatives in modern America continue to regularly use propaganda as a way to control the people and keep them in constant fear of something or someone. In the 1990s, conservatives in control of Congress attempted to persuade Americans that they should fear the evil Chinese because the Communist regime in Beijing posed some kind of threat to our national security. Conservatives never really defined what that threat was but they created a lot of upheaval around several incidents between China and the United States. This included suspecting every Chinese American was spying for the People's Republic of China (PRC) to Al Gore allegedly receiving campaign donations from the PRC. When that plan did not pan out, conservative turned their attention to the Middle East with a new leader in the White House.

President George W. Bush and his cronies continually conflated the separate issues of Al Qaeda's attack on the United States with the unrelated Iraq War by suggesting that Saddam had cooperated with Osama bin Laden despite the well-known fact that Osama despised Saddam for being a nonbeliever that needed to be removed from power to make way for the Islamic super-Caliphate that Al Qaeda would usher into existence in the campaign to purify the Middle East.[7] The Bush Administration

---

[6] Id. at 57.
[7] See Bush Administration on Iraq 9/11 link BBC

constantly invoked the actions of Al Qaeda on September 11, 2001, in speeches about Iraq saying "they attacked us" or "we fight them there so we do not have to at home" in hopes of convincing the people to allow the conservative administration to do whatever it wanted because scared people do not ask questions. Scared people will not seek out the real justifications for governmental actions as they are too focused on their own fear.

Although the president later admitted that there was no link between Saddam Hussein and Al Qaeda but at that point the damage had been done as much of the public had been convinced otherwise and was willing to extinguish their own liberty through electronic surveillance and other invasive means in hopes that President Bush would be able to do the impossible; prevent all future terrorist attacks.[8] In achieving this incredible feat, the conservatives adopted one of Hitler's tried and true propaganda tools by coming up with a message and repeating it loud and long enough that it eventually became true in the minds of the listeners as they did not take the time to analyze it and seek out additional information to determine its veracity. This successfully instilled fear and hatred allows President Bush to continue to misuse our enlisted military personnel in Iraq and disrespect our Constitution with secret spying programs that target Americans and the adoption of the Patriot Act, which has led to the mismanagement of billions of taxpayer dollars in his quest for government of, for, and by the corporations. Promoting militaristic policies, however, is not the only thing that fascist regimes use propaganda for.

Fascist regimes also use propaganda to promote a so-called return to traditional values and/or a return to a fictitious glorious past. Societies are ripe for these sorts of messages during major economic crises and civil upheavals as many people are often looking for someone to blame for their situation and where there is some identifiable group, be they internal or external, fascist take the advantage of the situation. Often linked with this return to traditional values is the idea of the racial superiority of some group of individuals. For example, German Nazis wanted to return Germany to its glory days of past empires as Germany was believed to be at its best, meaning it was a strong and formidable world power. An aspect of this lunacy was that the purity of the German/Aryan race needed to be protected from degradation by inferior peoples; the state needed to encourage the "right" people to procreate to produce offspring to protect that racial purity. According the Nazis, this racial purity would result in a strong and vibrant people ready to rule the world by military force ensuring

---

http://news.bbc.co.uk/go/pr/fr/-/2/hi/americas/3119676.stm. Published September 18, 2003.
[8] See Bush rejects Saddam 9/11 link http://news.bbc.co.uk/go/pr/fr/-/2/hi/americas/3118262.stm. Published September 18, 2003.

that the inferior races provide the labor needed to maintain the empire as God intended.

American conservatives currently engage in, and have in the past engaged in, similar abhorrent propaganda when they yearn for the "good ole days" as it is often put. Their position is particularly clear on issues of racial discrimination or the alleged immigration problem. On the issue of race, many conservatives longingly and whimsically recall the days when segregation, de jure and de facto, was acceptable in the social order and society was all the better for it as exemplified by Senator Trent Lott's statement at Senator Strom Thurmond's birthday party, which will be discussed later. Prominent conservatives like former North Carolina Senator Jesse Helms believes that America would have been better off had the proponents of the Civil Rights Movement waited for white America to come around to the realization that segregation was wrong rather than have a "liberal" Chief Justice Earl Warren and his Supreme Court usher in forced change. Helms' position is not far from what conservative practice has been on Civil Rights issues in America.

While much of American history, as taught to American schoolchildren, focuses nearly exclusively on history from the perspective of the conquerors, the White Anglo Saxon Protestants (WASPs), conservatives become discombobulated when there are any attempts to recognize key events and persons important to people of color. Whether it was the passage of the Martin Luther King Jr. National Holiday, Black History Month, discussions about slave reparations, Native Americans' treaty rights (i.e. the Boldt decision), Japanese internment, conservatives have fought strenuously to prevent recognition of these important people and events. The mind of the conservative seems to be unable to handle more than one thing; conservatives do not realize that it is possible for an American to love her country but also recognize that the American past also harbors innumerable examples of wrongs and evils visited on Americans from Rosewood, Florida to the Massacre at Horseshoe Bend, Alabama to the takeover of Texas and the southwest United States from Mexicans. Perhaps this is because conservatives are implicated in many of these atrocities and Americans may realize that fact, which could spell the death of the conservative movement in America and be an admission that they have sought the votes of white supremacist in American elections.

Any discussion about the fascists' propaganda promoting a return to traditional values and the glorious past is subsumed within the overarching fascist principle of nationalism. Nationalism is a rabid form of patriotism where its proponents are caught up in the fervor of supporting their government's actions even when the government is making policies that are not only bad for the society but violations of domestic and international law. In the international context, nationalism promotes the interests of the one over the interests of the many. Nationalism will also lead a country to violate its own basic legal principles and traditions because of the specter of some perceived internal threat. On both of these charges, the fascists of Germany and Italy were guilty. Hitler and Mussolini invaded other countries' sovereign territory in violation of international norms that required state's to respect the territorial integrity of other states; in this instance, the invaded states were Poland (Germany), Czechoslovakia (Germany), and Ethiopia (Italy).

Domestically, both men imprisoned and murdered German and Italian citizens and non-citizens in violation of their countries' established due process requirements and other fundamental protections as well as persons in countries that they invaded; the groups included millions of Roma (Gypsies), German Catholics, Communists, Socialists, Poles, Ethiopians, Jews, and others. These legal and constitutional violations took place because a large percentage of these nations' populations believed that these men would return them (Italians and Germans) to their former greatness if they only serve the state. Hitler and Mussolini sold millions on the concept of the superiority of the German and Italian nations and the need for them to assert that superiority to claim their rightful place in the world. If fascist have been successful in instilling nationalist ideals in a country's people, the people will feel the need to serve the government rather than the government serving the people.

In the wake of the World Trade Center attacks, the Bush Administration consistently called on the evil deeds of Al Qaeda when promoting its plan to invade Iraq in 2003.[9] The administration saw this as a great opportunity to manipulate the fear and anger of the masses. Al Qaeda's successful attack scared most Americans into the position that the only way they could be safe is by allowing the president to have any powers necessary to provide security even if it meant surrendering their fundamental civil liberties. When government starts to grab for expanded power, theoretically the people and *their* media question the government's motives and reasoning. In this case, neither the people nor the media raised a hackle about the administration's assertions that Saddam Hussein's Baathist regime was connected to Al Qaeda. The Bush Administration and its conservative allies even went so far as to say if you are not with us you must be with the terrorists, which impliedly means that in order to be a good American you have to side with the government and not question its motives as it is simply trying to protect you. Otherwise you must be a

---

[9] The justifications for the war have been numerous ranging from either preventing weapons of mass destruction from falling into terrorist's hands, freeing the Iraqi people from a despot, or bringing peace and democracy to the Middle East despite the real reason being Iraq's oil reserves.

traitor who is assisting Al Qaeda in its attempts to destroy America.

As a result of this fear-mongering, the people allowed the Bush Administration to indefinitely detain hundreds of U.S. citizens and non-citizens without charges or a chance to challenge their detention, use electronic surveillance against Americans without warrants, and numerous other actions all in violation of America's fundamental law, the Constitution of the United States. Being a real American came to mean not questioning the government's motives during a national emergency, instead the people were programmed to believe that they should serve your government in addition to not questioning the government's motives. For working class Americans, service to the conservative-dominated government meant sending your children to die in foreign wars to increase the wealth of the petroleum industry and the military-industrial complex. Where ever there is an effective propaganda machine promoting nationalism the principle of militarism is not far behind.

Militarist states see the use of armed conflict, not diplomacy and policy making, as the principal way to resolve lingering internal and international disputes. Militarist states must raise and maintain large security forces, armies, and navies to achieve its policy goals. In order to do this, the people need to feel that service to the state is honorable and respected, which leads to millions volunteering for service rather than being conscripted to serve. This creates a professional military class in society that take on a role similar to that in ancient Sparta and Rome where national resources are pumped into military bureaucracies while other aspects of society like public works and services are foundering. In Sparta, for example, life for its citizens revolved around maintaining a permanent military organization that used much of society's resources, human and economic. Military training began for children in Sparta during their pre-teen years. Those who did not excel in military training were shunned while those who did were granted more privileges and rights in society. Roman society also operated under a militaristic paradigm in which all landowners were conscripted for military service for Rome and Julius Caesar rose to the top of Roman political life because of his military exploits on the battlefield eventually and, Caesar argued, begrudgingly taking on the role of dictator of the Roman Republic. He did it only because the people wanted his leadership because of some perceived threat their "freedom."

At its roots, fascism promotes the idea that there is "a natural hierarchy" in society led by an aristocracy of prophets and warriors.[10] As such, in militarist states there is no equal protection of the laws; therefore, there is no equal treatment of similarly situated individuals because the warrior class and its leadership are given greater rights in society.

---

[10] Laqueur, *Fascism*, 24.

Furthermore, other areas (education and infrastructure) in society are neglected while the military class becomes rich and powerful. In Rome, which was the inspiration of the early fascists, dictators, as mentioned earlier, occasionally took control of the republic in the interest of protecting the people from some suspected internal or external danger. In conjunction with nationalist propaganda, twentieth century fascists used violence to gain control of society and repress their political rivals in an effort to consolidate their power over the state.

In fascist movements, the use of violence and armed force against opponents often began internally as the fascists moved to take control of a nation. The leader of the modern world's first modern fascist state, Benito Mussolini, has been quoted as having said "[t]he Socialist ask what is our program? Our program is to smash the skulls of the Socialists."[11] This illustrates the lengths to which fascist will go to avoid engaging in civil discourse about public policy and engaging in military and political violence. Mussolini, in particular, employed both mass violence and hired assassins to deal with trade union leaders and other political parties' leaders. Italian fascists' mass violence consisted of controlling the streets with massive rallies of paramilitary thugs and by causing public disorder at their rivals' political assemblies.[12] It should be noted, however, that internal violence and paramilitary violence is usually the finale of a well-organized campaign of propaganda intended to spread some vitriolic message against some identifiable racial or political opponent as the cause of the country's perceived problems, which is also used for the justification for creating a secret security/paramilitary force to maintain internal safety. After addressing internal security, fascist regimes often turn their attention to the international community for the redress of their grievances.

As history shows, Hitler targeted long lists of so-called undesirables for imprisonment, slavery, or annihilation using his Gestapo and SS to lead the charge on the home front. Internationally, Germany flexed its military muscle by seeking to right the wrongs that occurred in the aftermath of World War I with the Allies forcing Germany to cede its territory. The proposed solutions to these perceived internal and external security crises included ridding the world of all people of the Jewish faith and Germany reclaiming her lost territories and her place in the world by creating a strong military force. The plan was put into motion with the invasion of Czechoslovakia and Poland and the passage of repressive laws to confine Jews to ghettos and restrict their other activities, which eventually led to the concentration camps and death chambers.

American conservatives have adopted militarism as a central part of

---

[11] Id. at 50.
[12] Id.

their ideology just as the twentieth century's fascist regimes did including the use of internal forces (de jure and de facto) to suppress their rivals, which is promoted through the use of fear-based propaganda. Since Al Qaeda's spectacularly evil terrorist attack on September 11, 2001, conservatives have been especially shrill in their propagandistic promotion of fear among the American people. Terror alerts were raised frequently based on non-credible, non-specific, and unsubstantiated "threats" of terror attacks. This caused many Americans to abandon any criticism of the Bush Administration because it would either be seen as unpatriotic to criticize the government in a time of crisis as illustrated by former White House Press Secretary Ari Fleisher's warning to administration critics that "It reminds all Americans that they need to watch what they say, watch what they do"[13] in response to comedian Bill Maher's saying that the terrorist hijackers were not cowards and that Americans were the cowards for lobbing cruise missiles from thousands of miles away as if the First Amendment was suspended after the September 11 terror attacks or people were distracted by the threat of receiving anthrax in the mail and government advice to by plastic and duct tape to "protect" their homes from any biological and/or chemical weapons that Al Qaeda and its sympathizers may use next. In this melee, the people received the Bush Administration's message loud and clear; the message was that terrorists are lurking around every corner and the only way to stamp them out is to allow your president to the authority to secure the homeland and use resolute military force wherever they are.

Additionally, this caused Americans to alter their normal behavior as well as become suspicious of their neighbors and of course the Bush Administration attempted to take advantage of that suspicion. Then Attorney General John Ashcroft asked Americans to begin to spy on one another and report "abnormal" or "unusual" activity to the government under the TIPS program. If your neighbor altered his or her routine you should report it to the Federal Bureau of Investigations (FBI) so that it could be checked out because it may be another Al Qaeda sleeper cell that Osama bin Laden activated with a coded message that was aired by the news media. Together, these actions represented the Bush Administration's preparation of the American people, through the use of propaganda, for an internal and external military campaign to hunt suspected "terrorists" and sympathizers around the world.

Internally, the administration's critics would be ostracized and stymied in their attempts to call the government to account with the assistance of the "liberal media" leading to a near uniform falling in line of most Americans and those that did not were investigated as terror suspects.

---

[13] CNN's Reliable Sources, Are Journalists Jumping on the Bush Bandwagon, Aired October 6, 2001, http://www.cnn.com/transcripts.

For example, local police department's all across America infiltrated peace organizations opposed to going to war in Iraq with undercover police officers in search of suspected terrorists because, as believed by many, no good American would oppose the war in Iraq. Externally, the administration had the support and sympathy of much of the world, including Iran, in the aftermath of the attacks so when the United States began mobilizing forces to go after Al Qaeda in Taliban governed Afghanistan there were very few complaints from other nations. In fact, NATO actually exercised, for the first time ever, the treaty clause related to mutual defense of an attacked ally (an attack on one is an attack on all provision) making the Afghanistan invasion a truly multilateral military action. With these feathers in its cap, the Bush Administration quickly began to move forward their plans to remove Saddam Hussein from power in Iraq even against wide international disapproval including American allies like France who were fighting alongside U.S. forces in Afghanistan.

The propaganda campaign to sway the public to support his military misadventure in Iraq was solidified with over sixteen months of conditioning the public that Al Qaeda was in Iraq. Its success is evidenced in the lack of support by the majority of Americans for the Bush Administration before September 11, 2001 and the fact that by March 2003 a slight majority of Americans supported Bush's efforts to go to war in Iraq believing Saddam Hussein possessed weapons of mass destruction that were intended to target the United States and that Al Qaeda had ties to the infidel Saddam Hussein.

Remember that before the World Trade Center attacks, the Bush Administration was extremely unpopular among the American people. Thousands of spectators booed and threw objects as the presidential motorcade passed through the streets of the District of Columbia. In fact, Bush had to wear body armor in order to conduct the traditional walk down Pennsylvania Avenue and Laura Bush did not accompany him; this was quite different from the victorious stroll that President and Mrs. Clinton took down Pennsylvania Avenue on two prior occasions. Bush was chided for his failure to stay in Washington, D.C. during the summer of 2001 to deal with the failing economy as he, instead, spent tremendous amounts of time on vacation at the Bush family compound in Maine and at his Texas ranch. Nevertheless, the Bush Administration was able to use the September 11 attacks to their advantage and garner popular support with their propaganda for its military campaign in Iraq but it did not do it all by itself.

The conservative regime also received propaganda promotion assistance from talk radio and Fox News. Conservative talking heads like Rush Limbaugh and Glenn Beck promoted the Iraq War to the masses as necessary to stop an imminent nuclear attack on the United States by

Islamic terrorists. Conservatives talk show personalities, on radio and television, also attacked celebrities, or so-called "Hollywood Liberals," for speaking out against the Bush Administration's policies with taunts of "just shut up and sing." This implies that celebrities should simply entertain and not espouse their views on the political, social, economic, and environmental issues facing America regardless of the fact that conservatives waste little time in electing body builder-turned-actor Arnold Schwarzenegger, singer Sonny Bono, and actor Ronald Reagan with nary a word about their political activities. Another real fear that conservative talk show personalities harbor against celebrities speaking out is that they have equal access to the microphones and television screens of America and are often articulate enough to pose a serious threat to nonsensical conservative policies. They only want to hear from those celebrities they agree with as illustrated by the fact that B-movie actress Bo Derek's regular appearance at conservative events. With the assistance of conservative talk show personalities, the administration successfully indoctrinated millions of Americans to their cause. A side effect of all of this propaganda was that conservative viewers became riled up and ready to engage in violence and disorder for their cause.

Under the influence of heavy doses of propaganda, rank-and-file conservatives (i.e. American Brownshirts) went on a campaign to punish celebrities for engaging in their First Amendment right to speak out on political issues. Brownshirts lashed out at the Dixie Chicks' lead singer Natalie Maines for her declaring her views of President George W. Bush during a concert in the United Kingdom leading some conservatives to smash their CDs and burn concert tickets. In Las Vegas, Linda Ronstadt, while performing at a casino, had several members of an audience scream obscenities and destroy hotel/casino property all because she dedicated the song "Desperado" to documentary filmmaker Michael Moore. The then casino owner blamed Ronstadt for the melee despite audience members being responsible for the actual destruction. Finally, Slim Fast ended its endorsement relationship with Whoopi Goldberg because she made jokes about President Bush at a **private** Democratic Party fundraiser that they "heard about." Aside from these high profile cases, there are cases of some average Americans losing their jobs for heckling the president at rallies and even being arrested by law enforcement for wearing an anti-Bush t-shirt to a Bush campaign rally. These examples illustrate the extent to which conservatives have successfully infected the American psyche with the poison of un-Americanism; rank-and-file conservatives are only responding to the bell that has been rung by their ideological leadership like Pavlov's dog when they try to stamp out speech that they disagree with. The use of propaganda did not end with the start of the Iraq War in 2003 because the Bush Administration needed more troops to fight the war.

In the tradition of Hitler, the Bush Administration promoted the war on terror to America's young people by fabricating facts involving American service men and women as a way of recruiting more young Americans to go to war. In particular, the "liberal media" assisted the Bush Administration in advancing fabricated accounts surrounding the death of former NFL defensive back Pat Tillman and the capture of Jessica Lynch. Despite having knowledge that Pat Tillman lost his life as a result of friendly fire, the Bush Administration had a national memorial service in which they continued to state the claim that Tillman had died fighting Taliban forces in Afghanistan even though they knew the before the event took place that was not the truth. Even more egregious, the Bush regime used the nationally televised memorial service for Mr. Tillman as a recruiting opportunity although Mr. Tillman had previously refused to engage in any recruiting for the U.S. Army on numerous occasions according to his brother and other family members.

In the case of Jessica Lynch, the U.S. Army released information to the media claiming that Ms. Lynch had fought off Iraqi troops until her firearm had jammed and the Iraqis took her as a prisoner of war. The truth was that Ms. Lynch was severely injured in a vehicle accident when her unit had come under heavy fire from advancing Iraqi forces and several individuals in her vehicle were killed by the Iraqi troops. The Iraqi troops, then, turned the injured Lynch over to a civilian Iraqi hospital and left her there unguarded despite the U.S. Army staging an alleged rescue of Ms. Lynch from the hospital where she was given satisfactory treatment for her injuries by the Iraqi medical staff.

As with the alleged Gulf of Tonkin incident, the falsification of these incidents were intended to arouse a sense of patriotism in Americans with the result being that many Americans enlisted in the armed forces. The result has been that several hundred thousand Americans have suffered unnecessary injuries as a result of Bush's war in Iraq. Not only does militarism cost in lives and mental/physical disabilities, it destroys an entire generation's faith in the American system. Many young Americans went off to war believing they were fighting to protect America but later learned that they were simply pawns in the advancement of some corporatist's agenda to control Iraq's oil reserves. While the recruiting of America's youth to fight these foreign military escapades is one of the adverse results of militarism, it is by far not the worst.

While the Romans and Spartans had a professional military class that ranked near the top of their societies, the American conservative has created a professional military-industrial complex. Under this regime, corporate defense equipment manufacturers have effectively taken control of congressional committees responsible for defense appropriations as well as the Department of Defense with results being tens of billions of taxpayer dollars being handed over to these corporations. In exchange, the corporate defense manufacturers donate millions to the campaigns of representatives and senators for their votes on the legislation as well as hiring retired generals and other officers as lobbyists to use their contacts at the DOD to encourage its officials to support their pitches to congressional committees of new defense systems.

In fact, the power of these corporations is greater than the DOD leadership because even when they make specific requests for certain equipment and hardware that are in opposition to the corporate defense equipment manufacturers, the corporations still get what they want. For example, in 1995, the Republican controlled Congress forced the Air Force to accept two B-2 Stealth Bombers despite not needing or wanting them while the Navy's desperately wanted Seawolf Attack Submarine was cancelled because a conservative Congressman wanted the B-2 to be built in his district and he had the stroke to make it happen.[14] In fact, Air Force officials specifically requested, in a congressional hearing, that the money for the B-2s be transferred to the Navy for the building of the Seawolf Submarine but the B-2 manufacturer had provided enough campaign money to the right congressmen that it did not matter what the military brass wanted. This professional military-industrial complex is responsible for several hundred billion dollars being siphoned off from the American federal budget. It is also responsible for trillions of dollars of the national debt exemplified by failed programs like President Ronald Reagan's Strategic Defense Initiative (SDI) also known as Star Wars.

Despite Republican President and former Allied WWII Commanding General Dwight D. Eisenhower's warning of not to allow for the military-industrial complex to take control of the nation, Congress and the presidents have done just that. Even with the huge outlays from the national treasury to defense contractors the Bush Administration still sent thousands of U.S. military personnel into harm's way without body armor, with antiquated firearms, and with extremely low pay. That is perhaps the disgrace of conservative's ideology; they care more about corporate profits than they do our service members' lives. The people do not challenge this status quo because they have been strategically indoctrinated in the necessity of having a strong defense and never for one second acknowledge the need to question whether all of the equipment and hardware being purchased is necessary or even wanted by the military, which results in the ultimate success of the fascists internal plan to stifle all opposition.

Once fascists have gained control internally they turn their militaristic attention to other nations for the purposes of re-establishing

---

[14] See Eric Schmitt, "House Panel Backs B-2 But No Seawolf Subs," *New York Times*, May 24, 1995.

glory, regaining territories lost, and/or for natural resources not available in the homeland. Internally, militarism wreaks havoc on society but externally it creates a volatile world of arms races, high defense spending, and international mistrust and ignorance.[15]

When a fascist state focuses its militaristic policy toward other nations this implicates the principle of imperialism. Imperialist nations either seek to expand their territorial sovereignty or expand their economic/political hegemony over supposed inferior states and peoples. As illustrated previously, their willingness to use violence to gain power in their own countries underscores the extent to which they would go to achieve their international aims. Hitler's expansionist policies are well known but Mussolini's imperial ambitions are less known. Mussolini's expansionist policy focused primarily on Africa. In particular, Ethiopia was the target of the Italian Fascist leader's imperial policy leading to the death of tens of thousands of Ethiopians as the Italian military treated the people as if they were nothing more than insects by using poisonous gases against civilian populations.

Imperialism has been known to have severe side effects on local populations. In the late 18th and early 19th centuries, local peoples throughout Africa and Asia were forced to work as slaves gathering natural resources for shipment back to the colonial power's homeland for exploitation, not allowed to participate in the governing of their own societies, and treated as less than human by the so-called civilized peoples. Not only are colonial people subjugated and treated as mere servants to the colonial powers but, in many instances, they begin to believe they are inferior to the conquering powers. As many noted historians have pointed out, Japanese success on the battlefield and their utter brutality against Allied forces during World War II reversed this inferiority complex that the European imperialists had fostered in Africa as well as Asia and the Pacific Islands. As colonial peoples saw that the Europeans were not superior to them and that they could be defeated, independence movements against European imperialists sprang up all over the globe; from French territories in French Indochina (Vietnam) and Algeria to British territories in British India and Zimbabwe.

While these independence movements are generally a good idea because oppression anywhere in the world is unacceptable. In the meantime, colonial societies have been stunted in their economic, political, and social growth as millions of peoples were relegated to providing raw materials to Industrial European societies and treated as merely company

---

[15] From what I saw on American television as a boy, I believed that the Middle East was a dangerous place for Americans but after traveling there and meeting the people I learned that it was actually a safe place with friendly people.

towns and have no real practice with actual self-governance. Without practical experience, coups and civil wars have tended to dominate the post-colonial history of many of these countries. This is yet another horrendous side effect of imperialism. American conservatives have also engaged in imperialistic activities in the United States.

During the colonization of the United States by the British, and then the United States, Native American tribes were dispossessed of their native territories through the use various tricks and acts of unjustified warfare that amounted to, as post-revolutionary Americans saw it, an attempt to exterminate an infestation. In fact, one of the chief reasons, not mentioned in the Declaration of Independence, for going to war with Britain was the Royal Proclamation of 1763. The Proclamation prohibited white settlements from expanding westward into Indian Country in the interests of peaceful coexistence with the aboriginal peoples of North America not mention the British treasury had nearly exhausted its funds fighting the French and Indian War. Angered by this territorial limitation, many squatters and land speculators violated the royal edict by moving west and began to agitate for independence when the British Crown attempted to enforce the proclamation.

After the Revolutionary War, the new American government fully implemented manifest destiny by allowing white settlers to go into Indian country staking claims with no legal right to do so. President Thomas Jefferson, an avid Francophile, entered into an agreement with the French government to purchase land claimed by France west of the former British North American colony, which became known as the Louisiana Purchase. Jefferson, wanting to know the extent to which white settlements could expand, hired Meriwether Lewis and William Clark to survey the territory and file a report detailing their findings. After reporting the extensive number of Indian tribes they encountered between Missouri and the Pacific Ocean, the United States adopted a policy that sought to eradicate Native Americans as tribal entities and as Indians through the adoption of policies like allotment and termination up until the Nixon Administration adopted an official policy of self-governance for American aboriginals. In fact, a key part of government policy was to turn the Indian into productive white people. Before the Nixon Administration's official policy change the government officially wanted to make Native Americans into good white people. American imperialism has not been exclusively limited to the North American continent.

In the wake of the European scramble for Africa at the end of the nineteenth century and colonization of Asia, American policymakers saw the economic benefits derived from colonization for the Europeans and attempted to get in on the act themselves. After the *U.S.S. Maine* exploded and despite a later investigation showing that the explosion was an accident,

U.S. government officials had Congress declare war against Spain for allegedly bombing the *Maine* that led to America taking possession of the Philippines, Guam, Puerto Rico, and Cuba as colonies as prizes of war. It was the new Pacific territories that put the United States on a collision course with the Empire of Japan whose own territorial expansion in Asia quelled any further American expansion in Asia. For a period of about 30 years, Japan sought to eject European powers from Asia as the Land of the Rising Sun wanted to control the whole of Asia and its vast natural resources. Of course the tension between Japan and the United States came to a head at Pearl Harbor and throughout the Pacific as Japan took control of British and American territories like the Philippines.

Since then American imperialism has transformed from being entirely focused on military control of geographic territory to one focused on economic control of the globe through its hundreds of multinational corporations with headquarters in the United States but with its factories and warehouses in developing countries where workers are exploited and environmental standards are ignored in the interest of increasing profits for shareholders while the United States government serves as the envoy for these corporate interests in the international community. It is this economic imperialism that has been endorsed by conservatives in America that has sullied the reputation of the American people. People in developing countries suffer under unbearable conditions created by the American multinational corporations that represent this economic imperialism because, as previously mentioned, these multinational corporations receive special operating rights in developing countries that either do not have any labor/environmental regulations or are encouraged not to enforce those regulations. From Peru and Ecuador where oil sludge is dumped into fishing streams destroying the subsistence living of tens of thousands of people and poisoning the world's largest supply of fresh water in the Amazon River to China where workers have few protections and very unsafe working conditions leading to a high incidence of deaths and serious physical injuries in the workplace with no social safety net to help pick up the pieces.

While conservatives in America pay lip service to the promotion of liberty and democracy in the rest of world, their actions bear out another sad ideological reality; they support the spread of economic imperialism. In fact, former presidential candidate Rudy Giuliani stated in 2007 that unfettered capitalism is the best way to protect the people during a Republican presidential debate on the topic of economics at the University of Michigan-Dearborn. One would think that this allegedly educated man failed his high school American history class because he obviously does not remember the damage done to the American economy and the American people by unfettered a.k.a. laissez faire capitalism during the presidential administrations of Harding, Coolidge, and Hoover. Banks gave unsecured loans to big businesses to speculate in the stock market leading to a huge bubble of unrealistically high stock prices. When the bubble burst, big businesses collapsed as the stock prices fell, in turn big business had to layoff employees in droves, former employees could not withdraw money from banks to pay their debts or feed their families as banks closed their doors to prevent all deposits from being withdrawn while at the same time banks could not collect on the bad loans they had made to big businesses. This was a real domino effect.

American conservatives ignore this period in our history as it does not jib with their irrational philosophy of extolling the virtues of capitalism and virtually rewriting history as it relates to the failure of the unfettered market and how it hurt poor and working class Americans. Unemployment was believed to be nearly 25% as a result of corporate malfeasance but some historians believe that it was even higher. Conservatives would never admit that it was President Franklin Delano Roosevelt's response to the Depression created by corporate America was responsible for the large middle class that arose in the 1950s. Proof of that fact is that the conservatives effectively had no power in American government from 1932 until the early 1950s, around the time that American wages and the standard of living steeply climbed. Based on this period in American history, it has been shown that with private businesses focus being on the bottom line the government focus should be on shielding the masses from the adverse effects of capitalism. This brand of imperialism cripples national governments from responding to the needs and wants of local populations but instead demands that national governments bend to the will of the American multinational corporation. Economic imperialism has led to union organizers being murdered in Colombia and tens of thousands of Americans being poisoned in Anniston, Alabama. Economic imperialism cannot exist in a fascist state without the support of the power of the state; the state lends its authority to the business elite and/or provides special protections to chief business enterprises by entering into a symbiotic relationship with industry known as corporatism. This is done by conservative politicians who misuse public resources to promote the private interests of the business elite to the detriment of all.

Unlike its polar opposite on the political spectrum Communism, fascism does not seek to have industry owned by the masses through the organ of the state; instead, industry is expected to provide the state with whatever raw materials and manufactured goods it needs in exchange for the right to continue to operate privately with little governmental interference in business operations as well as receive exclusive government contracts. Hitler and Mussolini banned trade unions in the wake of their rise to power because the unions were seen as aligned with their sworn enemies, socialists and Communists. Business enterprises under both regimes received the benefit of not having to negotiate with workers on wages and other issues. This led to many abuses for workers as well as the displacement of some workers when German Jews were forced to work as slaves for some German businesses.

American conservatives have taken many of the same positions as the fascists of Germany and Italy. During America's historic expansion into the west, conservative governments seemed to side with big industry over the will of the people. One of the most heinous examples in American history is the government (i.e. U.S. Army) forcibly removing ranchers, farmers, and entire towns using its inherent eminent domain powers to condemn private property of individuals and turning that property over to railroad corporations. Another more contemporary example of government collusion with big business has been Verizon, the second largest cellular phone service provider in the country. In October 2007, Verizon admitted to Congress that it has turned over tens of thousands of customer phone records to the Bush Administration under the infamous and unconstitutional warrantless electronic surveillance program in exchange for exclusive government contracts to provide cellular phone service to federal employees. Additionally, the conservative Bush Administration's relationship with many large corporations has resulted in billions of dollars of public funds falling into the hands of corporate elites that just happen to be close friends of Administration officials and donors to their campaigns. With Halliburton and Blackwater USA being prime examples, many private corporations have received government contracts worth billions of taxpayer dollars to either (1) do work that can be done by government employees cheaper (but in line with the conservative attack on all things done by the government) they would rather contract it out at a cost to the American people than admit that government can do things cheaper and better than private industry or (2) do shoddy or little work (i.e. LSU developed New Orleans evacuation plan ignored as one purchased from private business that never produced the plan as demonstrated in the aftermath of Hurricane Katrina).

American conservatives even try to export their corporatist model to the rest of the world further promoting the infamous economic imperialism that sullies America's reputation. As previously mentioned, American corporations that operate their plants, factories, and warehouses in developing countries often receive special operating rights from those developing countries' governments. This is largely with the assistance of the United States government State Department and Department of Commerce that pressure economically strapped governments into giving concessions to private American corporations in the area of labor and environmental regulations at the expense of the local people. Ultimately, the relationship between these business entities and the administration raise numerous ethical and legal questions internationally and domestically. Conservative corporatism advances this idea that government's chief responsibility is to promote the interests of private industry over the desires and aspirations of the people. The number one way in which a conservative government can achieve this end is to intoxicate the people with a brand of religion that is fanatical and uncompromising, which leads to the final pillar of fascism.

As it relates the pseudo-religion principle, German and Italian fascism sought to create a version of Christianity that was subservient to the State but at the same time advanced the notion that their nations (i.e. ethnic group) were the chosen people of God. In Hitler's Germany, the Catholic Church was reviled by the regime and many Catholics were imprisoned, tortured, as well as killed by the Nazis (i.e. Night of the Long Knives). Hitler sought to elevate a version of Protestant Christianity that promoted his message of divine racial superiority for his Aryan race as opposed to the Jews were caricatured as demonic beings working for Satan. Many American conservatives have engaged in this fundamentalist, racial-religiosity as well.

Historically, it has been white society's justification for slavery and segregation as the Bible, God's word, endorsed these approaches (i.e. slaves being good to your masters and the Tower of Babel). Conservatives advanced this idea that Africans were of low mental aptitude with body's designed solely for physical labor under the guidance of strong white Christian leadership. This fundamentalist, some would say Jihadist, conservative version of Christianity also attempted to justify the extermination of Native American nations because they were considered heathens who did not believe in God and that God wanted white civilization to come to America so that the land would no longer lay fallow as God wanted the earth and its resources to be exploited, which was a common viewpoint of European settlers who conquered lands on other continents in the 17th, 18th, and 19th centuries.

Modernly American conservatives have attempted to spread their fundamentalist religious views using the instrument and authority of the state. On issues ranging from forcing children to pray in public schools to giving taxpayer dollars to alleged faith-based charities that will discriminate in who they give assistance to, to funding religious-based charter schools with public funds, conservatives have declared a clear intent to establish a radical Taliban like regime in America. Just as Hitler mistakenly declared Germans to be God's chosen people, American conservatives venture down the same divisive and violent path, which suggests that God hates the rest of the world and only loves Americans. In fact, some conservatives say things like "they deserved it" when natural disasters occur in other parts of the world like the Tsunami of December 2004. Pat Robertson famously talked about God punishing the people of Southeast Asia because of their ungodliness.

At this point, it has clearly been established that the conservative movement in America has fascistic tendencies as all of the key pillars of fascism are present in today's conservative movement and has deep roots in that movement historically. Traces of these fascistic principles will be self-evident as this book explores each of its carefully selected subjects. This discussion leads into the theme of this book: the death of liberty. Fascism is inherently anti-liberal. As a result of that bias, American conservatives have tended to attack the basic foundation of the American republic. At times, American conservatives sound more like Taliban and Iranian theocrats than they do real Americans. The chief goal of this book is to point out the dangers of conservatism. Many Americans identify with themselves as conservative without any examination of what the history of that movement has been in America and how it not only threatens people of color but also threatens all liberty.

This book will explore the conservative movement's plan for theocratic/plutocratic government in several different areas. The intent is to establish that American conservatism is un-American. It is un-American because it seeks to revoke those fundamental principles mentioned earlier as will be discussed in specific examples. For example, we will examine how conservatism seeks to dismantle Americans' understanding and support for civil liberties by suggesting that if you are not doing anything wrong what do you care if the government violates your rights by listening to your phone calls or reading your emails in Chapter III. The Anti-Federalists opposed the Constitution largely because it did not include protection of specific liberties shielded from governmental interference and control and demanded that it be amended to provide for such liberties. The Federalists initially argued that it was unnecessary to amend the Constitution because the new national government did not have authority to interfere with certain liberties as it was not in the Constitution but the first order of business of the First Congress was to amend the Constitution to include the amendments now known as the Bill of Rights. Our Founding Fathers did not trust government and neither should we. Modernly, conservatives make it seem as if the Bill of Rights is unnecessary. They talk about expanding government power with the stated goal of national security and safety despite the expansion being incongruent with the fundamental law of this country.[16]

---

[16] Even more outrageous is the general disdain with which conservatives view civil liberties. Conservatives generally refer to civil liberties as "technicalities." They never mention that many of the Founding Fathers, whom they claim to revere so

This book will also discuss, in Chapter IV, the issue of how American foreign policy has been hijacked by a cadre of conservative ideologues for the purposes of expanding the power of multinational corporations and the wealth of the American elite despite the broader effects of this policy on America and its citizens both at home and abroad. Next, the close relationship between conservatism and white supremacy will be analyzed in Chapter V. The goal here is to establish the fact that conservatism is intended to divide people along racial and ethnic lines to prevent the economic, social, and political progress of people of color but also of the poor white working class. Finally, we will turn to a discussion of the extremely important constitutional concept of judicial independence. The reader will discover that judicial independence is the chief means through which to maintain the Rule of Law, which prevents government from making arbitrary decisions in violation of the Constitution. However, first, in chapter II, this book will focus on the conservative war of theocracy. In particular, religious conservatives in America seek to impose a regime similar to that which governs Iran and that governed Afghanistan under the Taliban by destroying the basic tenets upon which America was founded.

---

much, thought that it was very important to amend the U.S. Constitution to guarantee that things that took place before and during the Revolutionary War under the old regime of King George would never happen again (e.g. unreasonable searches and seizures, forced self-incrimination, and inability to confront your accusers just to name a few). Civil liberties protect us all whether we are engaging in illegal activity or not. They are the backbone for maintaining a society in which the sovereignty flows from the people not from those who govern. Conservatives inherently believe in governance by the elites.

CHAPTER 2: AN AMERICAN THEOCRACY: THE REVOLT AGAINST OUR PLURAL LIBERAL DEMOCRATIC REPUBLIC

Since the founding of this great republic, the American conservative has espoused a version of religion that is hostile to America's fundamental principles of pluralism, liberty, democracy, and the sovereignty of the people by advancing the untenable notion that the Founding Fathers did not support the separation of church and state. On this point, conservatives have never presented any hard evidence to support their claim. Instead, they engage in the use of clichés by proclaiming that God had a hand in the formation of the American republic. The chief argument used by conservatives to support this tenuous statement is that the Founding Fathers were Christian. The problem with this overly simplified and ignorant statement is that it avoids any discussion of the history surrounding the adoption of the Constitution of 1787 and the Bill of Rights in 1791. Did the Founding Fathers want America to be a nation in which Christianity occupied a central role in government and society or did they want a society where all persons of all religious faiths (or no faith) could believe or practice as they wished with little or no governmental interference?

If you watch any of the "liberal media's" news reports, one would be led to believe that the answer to that question is unclear. However, an examination of the historical record reveals that the Founding Fathers, those in attendance at the Philadelphia Convention and doing the majority of the work on the Constitution, wanted the latter. They wanted America to be a plural, liberal, democratic, republic as discussed in Chapter 1. However, America's modern religious conservatives, some would say religious fundamentalists, want the former. Religious conservatives, like the former Taliban government of Afghanistan or the religious clerics in charge of Iran, want to use governmental power to enforce their religious ideals and morals.

Religious conservatives are more concerned with teaching children Creationism, under the guise of Intelligent Design, rather than teaching children English grammar, reading, mathematics, biology, chemistry, and physics. Proponents of the sham that is Intelligent Design advance the notion that life is too complex for it to randomly mutate into the numerous different species. They also advance the position that they simply just want to have a fair airing of their beliefs side-by-side with Evolution in public schools. The problem with this point of view is that Intelligent Design is not science. It is the belief of a few foolhardy religious fanatics bent on teaching Creationism in public schools to advance their religious dogma. These Intelligent Designists have argued that the proponents of Evolution have tried to silence them by keeping them out of schools.

Notwithstanding the fact that the real reason many people fight to keep Creationism/Intelligent Design out of public schools is that we must protect the separation of church and state to insure that no single religious doctrine is directly or indirectly sanctioned by the government, science has always been open to the concept of questioning the hypotheses and theories as proposed by Darwin, Newton, and others while Christianity and Islam have historically and contemporarily been inflexible and closed to new concepts or innovations. It is the closed nature of religious beliefs that make them unappealing and dangerous in the hands of the State and incompatible with the openness of science.

It is religion's uncompromising and inflexible nature that stymies development of societies as evidenced by the Dark Ages and, modernly, the Middle East. Not until the Enlightenment did man experience dramatic growth in Mathematics, Biology, Chemistry, and Physics. Reincorporating religion into public education will only result in a return to a period of ignorance that may prove insurmountable for American society. For example, religious conservatives propose abstinence only sex education in public schools as the only solution to teen pregnancy and disease prevention. However, their position presupposes that teens will heed their message and not engage in sexual conduct with one another. Truth is teens will engage in sexual conduct and teaching abstinence as an option along with condom usage and birth control is the only way to inhibit the spread of a myriad of sexually transmitted diseases that will adversely affect teens' lives and the community. There exists the potential to have an HIV/AIDS epidemic on the scale of that which exists in many parts of Africa where 20-30% of the population is infected as a result of religious superstition and ignorance. In Uganda, sex education that includes teaching condom usage has substantially cut the rate of infection in that country. There is another danger in allowing religion into the public school system.

American schoolchildren are already falling behind the children of developing countries where math and science-based careers are increasing at break-neck speed; allowing religious dogma into these important institutions may only exacerbate the problem as they will attempt to teach children religious fantasy about the origins of man as opposed to scientific fact and theory as well as, most importantly, how to think (i.e. critical thinking). Religious indoctrination is the responsibility of parents not the State. In America, parents are free to teach their children any religious beliefs they see fit. Public schools, however, must focus on what is good for the secular society as a whole; that is public schools should focus on spreading the gospel of math and science not the gospel of Matthew and Luke.

Religious conservatives in America have more in common with the clerics who lead Iran or the former Taliban regime of Afghanistan than they do with the men who founded America. For example, American conservatives constantly complain about university professors teaching children so-called "liberal" ideas arguing that these professors should be removed from their positions because of some perceived liberal bias. These professors discuss ideas like social justice, environmental protection, and American foreign policy failures just to name a few of the areas that send conservatives on fanatical tirades about how liberals hate America. Similarly, according to the Washington Post, the President of Iran recently announced that he wants to purge "liberal" professors from Iran's major universities. For the same reasons as American conservatives, the conservative Iranian president wants do away with the principle of academic independence; both want to control the information that reaches their nations' youths and inhibit free thinking as it may result in the overthrow of the regimes that benefit the continued ignorance of its populace.

For progressives and true liberals alike, the difference between Iran and the United States is that America was founded by men who were children of the Enlightenment; an age when established traditions and conventions, including religion, were challenged as new discoveries were made in the natural sciences and social sciences that contradicted the teachings of the religious leadership as man began to think of new ways to see the world. This puts religious conservatives on the wrong side of American history. Essentially, religious conservatives want to create a theocracy in America; this is government by the laws of God (as interpreted by clerics claiming a divine right to rule from God). This group of clerics is led by the likes of Pat Robertson, Jerry Falwell, and James Dobson just to name a few of the men who have more in common with Taliban leader Mullah Muhammad Omar than they do with George Washington.

Many religious conservatives will say that the comparison of them to the Taliban or Iranian clerics is mean spirited and in correct. However, their positions on most issues show just how closely they are aligned with those Islamic right-wing fundamentalists. Religious conservatives' positions include:

- Teacher-led prayer in public schools[17] like the Maddrassa schools found throughout the Muslim world where children are indoctrinated in a right-wing brand of Islam that preaches exclusion and division

- Banning the teaching of the science of evolution unless it is taught in conjunction with creationism

- Requiring K-12 school students to say the "under God" portion of the Pledge of Allegiance even if they are not Christian[18] is similar to the Taliban's plan to require all Hindi people to identify themselves

- Paying for religious indoctrination using taxpayer funds through so-called faith-based organizations who will distribute economic aid by tying it to religious indoctrination like the Saudi Arabian government's funding of Maddrassa schools throughout that country

- Banning a woman's right to choose whether or not to have an abortion similar to the authoritarian People's Republic of China's one child policy that controls women's reproductive rights

- Preventing same-sex couples from enjoying the same rights as heterosexual couples by opposing the banning of discrimination against homosexual people in employment, public accommodation, and housing; and this type of discrimination is common in the Muslim world

- Censoring books, movies, and music based on their belief that the content is inappropriate as was the case in Taliban-ran Afghanistan and the Islamic Republic of Iran

- Promoting the "traditional family" in which women subjugate themselves and their opinions to their husbands so much so that they no longer have any independence[19]

---

[17] They hold this position despite the U.S. Supreme Court ruling that children may pray on their own time so long as school time is not set aside for such activities.
[18] A minister wrote the original Pledge of Allegiance without any mention of God. "Under God" was added to the Pledge of Allegiance during the 1950s by Congress during our standoff with the USSR, which proclaimed itself an atheist state.
[19] Conservatives are now promoting marriage as a way for women to get off welfare even if it means marrying into an abusive relationship.

While these positions are entirely inconsistent with the principles of pluralism, liberty, democracy, and republicanism, these conservative positions stem from one fundamental misunderstanding held by many religious conservatives. Conservatives erroneously believe that God had a hand in the creation of America and, as such, Christianity should have a central role in American society. Additionally, conservatives arrogantly believe that God somehow loves Americans more than any other people on this Earth.[20] These beliefs wrongly rely heavily on the fact that the overwhelming majority of the Founding Fathers were members of some Christian-Protestant denomination as well as the fact that Christian prayers took place at the opening of each day of the Continental Congress. While these are important facts, it shows a horrendously ignorant understanding of American constitutional history.

However, to support their use of government to impose their religious beliefs, religious conservatives needed some theory, no matter how tenuous, to support their efforts to forge ahead with creating a society that would operate under one groups' religious doctrines no matter what the real history consisted of. That theory is that Christianity was so interwoven into the fabric of American government and society during the founding of this great republic that they are inseparable. Even if that were true, they are sadly mistaken in believing that Christianity was granted some special position in America by the Founding Fathers.

First, the Founding Fathers did not give Christianity any special sanction in the U.S. Constitution. In fact, the U.S. Constitution never mentions God except at the end where it says "in the year of our Lord" when giving the date the document was signed which was a common practice in the 18th century carrying no religious significance. The fact that conservatives believe such a ludicrous premise proves not only their ignorance of the history of sectarian strife in Europe that so deeply influenced the Founding Fathers that many disavowed any attempts to commingle religious and civil affairs as will be later examined. It also proves that conservatives lack any understanding of level of religious acrimony and violence in the history of colonial British North America and post-Revolutionary America. The proof of the effect of the events in Europe and North America on the Founding Fathers and their desire to maintain a separation of church and state dominated the national debate over governmental authority.

---

[20] As a Christian, I am offended that the religious right would suggest that God had a hand in the near annihilation of millions of Native Americans and their societies and the enslavement of millions of Africans so that land hungry and money crazed white Christians could have the good life. Nevertheless, I am sure there are those people on the religious right who believe that.

The Founding Fathers learned from their own conflict-filled histories both in Europe and in America that religious strife can, and oftentimes did, destroy societies with sectarian divisions and civil war.[21] For example, Oliver Cromwell and his Roundheads beheaded English King Charles I because he was a Catholic ushering in the Long Parliament and a time of much division and uncertainty in that society. While this was not the most egregious example of sectarian violence in the United Kingdom or in Europe for that matter, it solidified an understanding in the minds the Founding Fathers that religious divisiveness was dangerous and could not be allowed to take root in the United States. Notwithstanding their Old World experiences with religious strife and civil unrest, the Founding Fathers also had experience with religious turmoil in the America's that further buttressed their understanding that combining civil and religious authorities under the same umbrella was a bad idea.

Popularly but mistakenly, many Americans believe that the individuals who colonized early Colonial America came here with the intent to establish a place where everyone could have religious freedom to believe and practice religion as they saw fit. However, that was not the case as the Puritans who left England in the 1600s to colonize North America were engaged in conflict with the Church of England because it was not changing as they thought it should (i.e. eliminating the last vestiges of its ties to the Catholic Church). The Puritans intended to come to North America to establish a religious society that could serve as an example to their rivals in England. These new settlements operated under councils that had legislative, executive, and judicial authority over civic and religious affairs. The councils controlled every aspect of colonists' lives from enforcing the rule of mandatory religious practice and observance (i.e. church attendance) to trying individuals suspected of practicing witchcraft.

The best example is the Massachusetts Bay Colony. The first thing that comes to mind when discussing the Massachusetts Bay Colony is the Salem Witch Trials. While those events are applicable and gruesome examples of religious tyranny and violence perpetrated by government officials, there are also less inflammatory examples that illustrate the ill effects (i.e. tyranny and oppression) of combining civic and religious authority under one umbrella. Many colonists simply bent to the will of the religious fundamentalists who governed Massachusetts Bay Colony for fear of being banished or put to death on some trumped up charge of heresy or witchcraft. Some, however, rose in the face of these threats to denounce the injustice of the civic authorities inhibiting religious freedom. One great American pioneer for religious liberty was Roger Williams who showed

---

[21] Remember Oliver Cromwell and his Protestant Roundheads crushed the predominately Catholic forces King Charles I.

courage in opposing the government's autocratic efforts to prohibit individuals from freely practicing their religion outside of the control of the State.

Roger Williams, a Protestant minister, led the fight in colonial America to prevent the expansion of theocratic regimes in the rest of colonial America so that colonists could worship, or not worship, as they saw fit. Williams, born in 1603 in England, was a graduate of Cambridge University where he studied to be a minister in the Church of England. While at Cambridge, Williams met other students who thought that the Church of England should abandon the last vestiges of Catholicism that remained a part of its rituals and traditions. These individuals who were known for their unrelenting desire to reform the church were called the Puritans. With attempts to reform the church failing in England and many Puritans facing arrest for their opposition to the church, some of these Puritans left on the *Mayflower* where they founded Plymouth Colony in Massachusetts in 1620.

Williams did not arrive in Massachusetts until 1631 where local officials greeted him as a "great minister."[22] Williams turned down the offer to be the minister at the new Puritan church in Boston because the church remained a part of the Church of England. Instead, Williams sought a position at the Salem church where the congregation clearly desired to separate from the established church. Williams did not become the minister of the Salem church as Boston officials used their considerable clout to ensure that Salem did not offer Williams the job. This led Williams to Plymouth Colony, which had formally separated from the church, where he served as their minister from 1631 to 1633. In 1633, after some deliberation, Williams returned to Salem with the intent to make a principled stand against the tyranny of the colonial civic/religious leadership.

Williams made his positions clear to the colony's leaders on the proper role of religion and civil government in society. Religion was a matter of one's conscience. A private matter that should be outside the scope of the government's control and influence. People had a right to worship what, when, who, and how they wanted or not at all. First, Williams made clear that no one should be forced to swear oaths to God as not everyone worshipped the Christian God. Next, Williams declared that public officials had no right to enforce religious responsibilities like tithing and religious observances. For example, Sabbath laws prohibiting certain activities on Christian holy days were violations of the principle of religious liberty. Finally, Williams pointed out that Christianity did not give the King

---

[22] Edwin S. Gaustad, *Roger Williams: Prophet of Liberty*, (New York: Oxford University Press, Inc., 2001), 14.

of England the authority to dispossess the Native American peoples of their land without just compensation and that engaging in such activity was the most ungodly activity a person could possibly do.

The Massachusetts General Court, which had legislative and judicial authority, called Williams forward to answer for these unpopular and illegal opinions on July 8, 1635. The body warned Williams to refrain from making such statements or suffer the consequences. However, Williams continued to publicly express his opinions on these matters leading the Massachusetts General Court to ask Williams to withdraw the statements on October 8, 1635. In the face of Williams' refusal to withdraw the statements on October 9, 1635, the Massachusetts General Court expelled Roger Williams from the colony giving him six weeks to leave.

With the deadline fast approaching and Williams neither withdrawing the statements nor leaving the colony, colonial officials planned to arrest Williams and send him back to England, where he would face even more relentless persecution at the hands of officials of the Church of England. Thanks to warnings from friends, Williams fled into the wilderness where he spent several weeks wandering aimlessly. Eventually, Williams settled on the Narragansett River on land he purchased from local tribes, which became the site of the city of Providence and the first settlement of Rhode Island. The importance of this colony cannot be overstated. It became a bastion for those who wanted to worship, or not, in their own way without interference from meddlesome government officials. Catholics and Protestants peacefully coexisted in this new colony. Williams even invited individuals with whom he disagreed to settle this territory. Williams' efforts strengthened the fledgling principle of religious liberty in colonial America by providing a place for it to flourish in the sight of so much religious tyranny.

Because of these experiences and Williams' efforts, the Founding Fathers supported a freedom of religion that meant little or no governmental interference with religious institutions, beliefs, and practices as well as vice versa. The intent was to prevent any unnecessary entanglement between the civil authorities and the religious authorities. The concept of separation of church and state began as early as 1066 when the Normans led by William the Conqueror won the Battle of Hastings taking control of England and created, for the first time, the courts of law separate from religious leaders and requiring the church to institute its own ecclesiastical courts for addressing religious disputes and issues.

With their European experiences of sectarian warfare and religious bloodshed in North America, the Federalist-controlled First Congress acceded to the Anti-Federalists' demands that the new Constitution be amended to place religion beyond the reach of the government despite the protestations of the Federalists that the government already had no authority over religious matters.[23] The Federalists and Anti-Federalists resolved their differences with the adoption of the Bill of Rights of 1791 after an intense national debate between the parties.

The Founding Fathers could be classified into two general categories; they were Federalist and Anti-Federalist. The Federalists were proponents of the Constitution as it was drafted at the Philadelphia Convention. This group included men like George Washington, Alexander Hamilton, John Jay, John Adams, John Marshall, and James Madison just to name a few. The Anti-Federalists either outright opposed the Constitution or thought that it needed to be altered to protect individual rights from a perceived encroachment that would occur because the Constitution gave too much power to the government. Anti-Federalists included Thomas Paine, Thomas Jefferson, Patrick Henry, and many other men who refused or were not invited to attend the Philadelphia Convention. These differences led to a public and, often, intense debate about government authority.

In the wake of the Constitution's drafting at the convention and its proposal by the Confederation Congress, one of the public debates about government power that took place between the two groups was whether the new national government had the power to act in the realm of religion under the Constitution of 1787. Those who believed that the new national government created by the Constitution of 1787 did not possess the authority to legislate on matters of religion were Federalist, exemplified by Alexander Hamilton and James Madison. The Anti-Federalists, who believed that a bill of rights was necessary to guarantee that the new national government would stay out of matters of religion, were led by Patrick Henry and Thomas Paine.[24] Thus, both sides believed that the national government should have no authority over religious matters. What the Founding Fathers disagreed about was whether the Constitution as written at the 1787 convention prevented the government from legislating in that realm or whether a bill of rights that included that specific prohibition was necessary. Turning to a closer examination of each sides' point of view, it will be easy to see that the modern conservative allegation that Christianity and the United States are somehow tied at the hip is easily refuted.

Representing the views of the Federalists is James Madison, the fourth President of the United States and drafter of the first proposed constitutional amendments from which we get the ten amendments that

---

[23] See Gary Wills, editor, *The Federalist Papers by Alexander Hamilton, James Madison, and John Jay*, (New York: Bantam Books, 1982), 434-443.
[24] The dispute was settled with the adoption of the Bill of Rights, which included the Establishment Clause and Free Exercise Clause.

became the Bill of Rights (1791).[25] Madison, like most of his
contemporaries, understood that the last thing a newly established nation
needed was religious strife of the kind so prevalent throughout Europe.
Religious strife often resulted in bloodshed in Europe and many Federalist
knew that the only way to prevent this strife from taking place in America
was by preventing the old political-religious order from taking root in
America.

The only true way that religious liberty can flourish in the United
States is by maintaining a strict separation between church and state. As the
original drafter and congressional sponsor of the amendments that later
became the Bill of Rights, Madison is in the best position to demonstrate
what the Founding Fathers perspective was on the issue of church and
state.[26] This is important because one of Madison's proposals to amend the
Constitution included what we now call the First Amendment, which
contains the Establishment Clause and the Free Exercise Clause. On June
8, 1789, Madison introduced the first draft of the Bill of Rights in Congress,
which included the following on religion:

> The civil rights of none shall be abridged on account of
> religious belief or worship, nor shall any national religion
> be established, nor shall the full and equal rights of
> conscience be in any manner, or on any pretext infringed.[27]

This was Madison's attempt to satisfy the desires of the Anti-Federalists by
putting matters of religion entirely in the private sphere rather than in the
public. Conservatives will argue the narrow point that the Establishment
Clause's only purpose is to prevent Congress from establishing a national
church. However, as shown by the original draft of what became the
Establishment Clause and the Free Exercise Clause as well as what will be
evidenced by a careful examination of Madison's other writings, one will see
that the conservatives' interpretation is erroneous and quite possibly
intended to mislead the American public to promote their mythology about
the role of Christianity in America.

As a delegate to the 1787 Philadelphia Constitutional Convention,
James Madison was one of the most active delegates as evidenced by his
extensive involvement in the drafting of the Federalist Papers, which were
intended to explain the contents and purposes of constitutional provisions
to the people of New York and their ratifying convention. Initially, the

---

[25] Jack N. Rakove, editor, *James Madison, Writings*, (New York: Literary Classics of
the United States, Inc., 1999), 467.
[26] Id. at 437-452.
[27] Id. at 442.

Federalists responded to Anti-Federalists complaints about the Constitution extending too much power to the national government by saying that if it is not enumerated then the government does not have authority over it. Eventually acquiescing to the Anti-Federalists, the Federalists proposed and the states ratified the 10 amendments that became the Bill of Rights to satisfy demands of the Anti-Federalists as previously discussed. During this entire debate, James Madison took the lead role on representing the Federalists' position on religion and the new national government.

Madison clearly, concisely, and repeatedly articulated a viewpoint that signaled the Federalists' unwillingness to engage in the past divisiveness that religion brought to society. When responding to Anti-Federalists' concerns about the new national government's authority over religious worship, Madison explained that Congress had no constitutional authority to either establish a national church or grant preferential treatment to a specific church because "[t]he government has no jurisdiction over [religion]."[28] Madison did not take this position simply because he wanted to satiate the Anti-Federalists; he wanted to clearly declare that the Constitution created a limited government in which matters like religion were beyond its control. The intended purpose of maintaining this separation was to protect the one from the other and vice versa.

Madison, like the majority of Federalists, believed that "religion and Govt. [would] both exist in greater purity, the less they are mixed together."[29] It is when the two are "mixed together" that oppressions of the minority and liberty occur. The primary result of creating any alliances or coalitions between government and religion is a "corrupting influence on both"[30] as exemplified by the goings on in the Massachusetts Bay Colony where Roger Williams were banished by the civil authorities for their religious beliefs as previously discussed. If state and church affairs are maintained separately, religious freedom would flourish because "all Sects might be safely & advantageously put on a footing of equal & entire freedom."[31] Furthermore, with all religious Sects being equal "no one sect will ever be able to out-number or depress the rest."[32] This was a very new and innovative concept that the Federalists were advocating as the Old World conservatives traditionally saw the state-church dichotomy entirely differently.

It was the Universal opinion of the Century preceding the

---

[28] Id. at 360-361.
[29] Id. at 789.
[30] Id. at 788.
[31] Id. at 789.
[32] Id. at 382.

last, that Civil Govt. could not stand without the prop of a
Religious establishment, & that the Xn. religion itself,
would perish if not supported by a legal provision for its
Clergy. The experience of Virginia conspicuously
corroborates the disproof of both opinions.[33]

Madison saw a stable state government in Virginia functioning with
great success and numerous independent religious sects practicing freely
and flourishing without an inkling of support one from the other. The
chief lesson to take away from James Madison is that the Founding Fathers
wanted the American republic to be a beacon of religious pluralism and
liberty to the world as Madison so eloquently states here:

We are teaching the world the great truth that Govts. do
better without Kings & Nobles than with them. The merit
will be doubled by the other lesson that Religion flourishes
in greater purity, without than with the aid of Govt.[34]

The American republic was not intended to be some backwater
theocracy governed by fanatical clerics like Falwell, Dobson, or Robertson.
Not only did Madison talk-the-talk; he also walked-the-walk.

Throughout his political career, Madison made many efforts to
prevent the re-creation of the political-religious entanglements that existed
in the Old World. In 1785, Madison wrote a letter to protest a bill before
the Virginia General Assembly proposing to fund teachers of Christianity.[35]
During Madison's First Inaugural Address, he included as one of his goals
as President of the United States "to avoid the slightest interference with
the rights of conscience, or the functions of religion so wisely exempted
from civil jurisdiction."[36] In 1819, Madison opposed the appointing of
chaplains by both houses of Congress at the expense of the taxpayers where
he asked "[i]s the appointment of Chaplains to the two Houses of Congress
consistent with the Constitution, and with the pure principle of religious
freedom? In strictness the answer on both points must be in the negative."[37]
The problem that Madison perceives, and rightly so, is that these chaplains'
pay will come out of the national treasury, which amounts to the funding of
religious worship.[38] It also creates the problem of inequality between and
among the various religious sects in that some will obviously not be

---

[33] Id. at 726-727.
[34] Id. at 789.
[35] Id. at 29-36.
[36] Id. at 681.
[37] Id. at 762.
[38] Id. at 762.

included for one reason or another.[39] The point here is not to restate Madison's every effort to protect religious liberty but to clearly establish that the author of the Establishment and Free Exercise Clauses of the First Amendment truly believed that we could create a society where there was true religious freedom. While Madison represents only one of the many Founding Fathers (despite his position as a leading convention delegate, author of the Federalist Papers, and the spokesman on the issue of religion for the Federalists) there were instances of the Founding Fathers nearly unanimously rebuffing attempts to create political-religious entanglements.

On June 28, 1787, when Pennsylvania Delegate Benjamin Franklin rose on the convention floor and said "I therefore beg leave to move, That henceforth Prayers, imploring the Assistance of the Heaven and its Blessings on our Deliberations, be held in this Assembly every morning before we proceed to Business; and that one or more of the Clergy of this city be requested to officiate in that Service."[40] This motion was defeated overwhelmingly with less than a handful of the delegates in attendance voting in favor of it.[41] This even after Franklin made a passionate appeal to the convention delegates that morning prayer to the "Father of Lights" could provide guidance to the assembly just as it had at the beginning of the struggle for independence from Britain. The overwhelmingly establishes that the Founding Fathers wanted to create a strong civil government with limited authority in its citizens' private affairs such as religion. This is entirely counter to the religious conservative's view that since the Founders were themselves Christians they would wholeheartedly support our federal government favoring Christian religious sects to the exclusion of all others. In fact, this example strikes at the very heart of one of the religious conservatives' core belief; that the law, especially the Constitution of the United States, by which we are governed comes from God.

Quickly recapping the decisive historical record: (1) the Federalists and Anti-Federalists argued about whether the Constitution as written sufficiently separated church and state not whether there should be a separation of church and state, (2) James Madison, author of the Bill of Rights, clearly identifies the need for a separation of church and state in his numerous writings on the subject, and (3) the Philadelphia Conventions' rejection of Benjamin Franklin's call to invoke his Christian God all clearly demonstrate the opposite view as that advanced by American conservatives.

American religious conservatives want the government to pick

---

[39] Id. at 763.

[40] J.A Leo Lemay, editor, *Franklin: Essays, Articles, Bagatelles, and Letters, Poor Richard's Almanack, Autobiography*, (New York: The Library of America, Literary Classics of the United States, Inc., 1987), 1138-1139.

[41] Id. at 1138.

winners and losers among religious denominations, which is at the crux of Bush's faith-based initiative. That decision should be left to individuals not government. Individuals should decide when to donate money to the religious institutions of their choosing, attend the religious services of their choosing, and indoctrinate their children in the religious beliefs and practices of their choosing. This is not the role of government. If a specific religious denomination becomes defunct as a result of the people having decided that that religious denomination is not worthy of their participation or donations, then that decision should be honored by government. That is to say, government should not provide secularly collected tax revenue to sectarian private organizations to prop them up.

The same holds true when a religious denomination flourishes. It will receive enough funding from its congregation that it will not have a problem surviving as the people have spoken by supporting an organization they consider worthy of their support and should not be given, nor does it need government assistance. Government should not be concerned with the survival of religious institutions as this is the job of the people individually. Conservatives seem to believe in the free market in all other aspects of American life except in matters of conscience and faith.

It is time we as Americans begin to reject religious conservatives' red herring assertions that religion has been removed from the public arena and that it somehow deserves a special status in society. Despite claims to the contrary, there is nothing, judicially or constitutionally, that prevents religious organizations from holding their worship services or publicly praying (i.e. in parks, in town squares, on city hall steps, and on sidewalks) when they want to. Nor is there anything preventing their children from engaging in prayer in public schools on their own. Our Constitution merely prohibits the government from forcing or mandating that everyone engage in these activities as conservatives would like. Government is intended to protect and serve all persons without regard to whether they are Jewish, Christian, Muslim, Buddhist, Hindus, or any other religious sect.

When matters of the conscience become concerns of the State, it becomes easy for the group in power to attempt to control and/or devalue the beliefs and practices of those individuals or groups different from their own. Religious conservatives attacks on academia, science, and free expression usually results in a society devolving into an abyss of economic and social stagnation as well as enforced ignorance, which appears to be where America is headed if conservatives are allowed to continue to using religion as a red-herring. As shown by our historical record, government should be strictly secular in its operation to insure that all citizens regardless of their religious heritage or lack thereof receive equal treatment. While this discussion is primarily concerned with the protection of religious liberty, conservatives have also historically and contemporarily assaulted America's other fundamental civil liberties under the guise of law and order as well as homeland security.

CHAPTER 3: CONSERVATIVES & THE DEATH OF AMERICAN CIVIL LIBERTIES

"In Virginia I have seen the bill of rights violated in every instance where it has been opposed to a popular current."[42]

James Madison 1788

The sentiment expressed by James Madison in 1788 continues to hold true today. Whenever a ruling majority is convinced that it is in their interest to violate the rights of others they will. That is why the Founding Fathers, led by former Continental Army Lieutenant and Chief Justice of the United States John Marshall in <u>Marbury v. Madison,</u> revolutionized our Constitution. For the first time in government, a constitution would be considered to be the law and not a political document that could be disregarded by the government as was common practice in the 18th century. In <u>Marbury,</u> Marshall declared that because the Constitution is the fundamental law of the land it is supreme to acts of Congress and the president and, furthermore, that it is the responsibility of the U.S. Supreme Court to decide what that fundamental law means. The overall effect of this ruling on future generations of Americans is that the people's civil liberties protected by the Constitution would be protected by the federal judiciary from the ever encroaching legislative and executive branches of government. The role of the judiciary in protecting our civil liberties will be discussed at length later in the chapter on judicial independence. For now

---

[42] Rakove, *James Madison, Writings*, 420.

we will focus on conservatives' perversion of the importance of our civil liberties.

Conservatives have had great success in convincing many Americans that constitutional civil liberties are merely technicalities used to get guilty criminals off and not important in everyday American life. Proof of conservatives' success in minimizing the importance of civil liberties is shown in the ease with which some Americans are ready cede their liberty to the government under the idiotic theory of "if I am not doing anything wrong, what do I have to worry about." This asinine theory has gained acceptance by some as exemplified in the U.S. Congress' adoption of the U.S.A. PATRIOT Act. The Bush Administration persuaded members of Congress that Americans' liberty could only be protected by having a strong national security apparatus in which Americans give up their liberty. To some people, this circular reasoning may seem rational but it is entirely ludicrous. If you are giving up liberty to the government you are not protecting liberty because your liberty is being diminished. The fact that Americans who identify themselves as conservative do not see the circular nature of that argument is a testament to the damage done to the American educational system by conservative national and state governments' under-funding K-12 education and other policies.

Instead of teaching Americans to be critical thinkers, our educational system has been designed on the idea of creating obedient, misinformed servants for the elite. This system propagates the myth of George Washington not telling a lie. However, most Americans, when asked, could not even tell you what a civil liberty is or give an example of one. While many Americans will readily say that flag burning should be made illegal, they cannot tell you that they live in a federal republic built on the principles of democracy, liberty, and openness (plural). Now, while I am an advocate for extensive reforms of K-12 education on a national level that is not the focus of this chapter. My purpose is to bring attention to the conservatives' success in advancing this circular argument for 'protecting-diminishing' liberty through more government power. Recognizing that members of the Bush Administration cannot be accused of being scholars, there is something more sinister amiss in this Rovian theory. Elite conservatives are protecting the ruling class by attacking and seeking to destroy true notions of liberty.

American conservatives have long proclaimed themselves the champions of liberty. However, conservatives have a long history of suppressing the liberty interests of others that includes a long list of racial and ethnic minorities, women, people with disabilities, and many others. For example, conservatives, not just southerners, prohibited African Americans and other people of color from voting, living in certain parts of town, working in certain professions, joining trade unions, marrying white

Americans, traveling through certain regions, and deprived them of their lives by engaging in the practice of lynching accused persons without any trial. The United States committed acts of genocide against Native American tribal nations in the white man's pursuit for their ancestral lands like the forced removal of the Cherokee from Georgia to Oklahoma Territory or the Creek War.

Even more brazen, elite white conservatives did all of this while simultaneously repressing the large poor white working class of the South and Midwest. On the one hand, they distracted poor and working class whites from the inequality of the system that held them back and protected the elite white aristocracy using racist messages that made it okay for poor whites to direct their anger and frustrations toward African Americans and other people of color while, on the other hand, allowing elite whites to maintain control over poor whites by discriminating against poor whites by preserving an inadequate educational system, low wages, and substandard housing ensuring that they would remain a largely illiterate, ill-informed mass of workers intended to maintain the white aristocracy's wealth. Whenever anyone attempted to challenge this divide-and-conquer strategy of white aristocratic dominance, they were immediately slapped down by the powers that be.

This was the case in the early 1900s when some southern farm laborers formed the biracial Southern Tenant Farmers' Union to challenge the power of elite southern white landowners who took advantage of poor African American and white sharecroppers with unfair land-lease agreements and prices for seed. When prominent landowners learned of secret meetings at which both African American and white sharecroppers were present, sheriffs would often raise a posse to attempt to arrest the attendees for breaking the time-honored Jim Crow law of participating in biracial meetings. This is a clear violation of these individuals' First Amendment right to freedom to peaceable assembly but southern conservatives wanted to maintain the order that preserved their wealth and status by keeping white and African American workers segregated.

Contemporarily, conservatives have continued and expanded their efforts to usurp the civil liberties of Americans. President G. W. Bush and other conservatives have expanded the power of the American presidency at the expense of the American people's liberty and sovereignty in ways that resemble what Adolf Hitler and his Nazi regime did in Germany as discussed in Chapter 1. In fact, since George W. Bush ascended to the presidency, he has sought to expand presidential power like no other president in an effort to create a monarchical presidency. His conservative administration has constantly and consistently attacked America's fundamental civil liberties and Congress, unlike past Congresses, seemed ill prepared to respond to his actions partially due to the president's own party being in control of Congress for 6 of his 8 years in office. As Congress failed to react or counterbalance the administration, Bush's cohorts grew more emboldened as time passed resulting the disclosure of Valerie Plame's identity to settle a political score with her husband former Ambassador Joseph Wilson. The administration's list of atrocities and malfeasance grew exponentially and are too numerous to mention in their entirety, but the following paragraphs chronicle the most ominous and egregious acts that counted among the daggers stabbed into the heart of the Constitution.

For example, the Bush Administration abandoned our international treaty obligations that prohibit the abuse of prisoners of war while simultaneously ignoring the U.S. Constitution's protections for accused persons. In international law, certain legal standards become so widely acknowledged and adopted that they become a part of international customary law, which generally means that no country is excluded from its application even if the country has not signed onto an international treaty agreeing to limit its authority under the treaty. Alongside genocide, it has long been an established custom in international law that captured enemy fighters would be classified as prisoners of war and treated accordingly.

However, the initial misstep of the Bush Administration occurred when Bush refused to recognize captured Taliban soldiers' status as prisoners of war by instead declaring them "enemy combatants" despite these men being members of the military of the then Taliban regime governing Afghanistan. Had these men been detained a POWs, pursuant to international law, the United States Armed Forces could detain these individuals for as long as hostilities exist between the United States and the Taliban without charges, which could potentially be years to come. This as well as other actions by President G. W. Bush created an environment where U.S. soldiers killed and maimed innocent civilians in Iraq as well as abused alleged insurgents/terrorists at Abu Graib and at Guantanamo Bay Naval Base. Some of the other wrongdoing undertaken by President Bush's regime include the National Security Agency engaging in warrantless electronic surveillance of Americans in violation of the Constitution, the president threatening to bomb Al Jazeera—the Arab world's only truly free press—because it does not support Bush's war effort and reports negative stories about his administration's failures in Iraq, the Department of Defense banning media coverage of the return of U.S. war dead from Iraq and Afghanistan, the Central Intelligence Agency employing a practice known as extraordinary rendition by kidnapping individuals suspected of supporting terror organizations off the streets of Europe and other parts of the world and placing them in so-called black sites, and, most importantly, President Bush signing into law the constitutionally questionable USA Patriot Act (the modern Alien and Seditions Act). We will talk about some of those examples in detail later on, but the cumulative effect of Bush's actions have spilled over to the broader society resulting in rabid, conservative Americans attacking other Americans for engaging in the time-honored right of free speech and free expression protected by the First Amendment by calling them un-American.

In Germany, when the Nazi Party was attempting to gain power and suppress its rivals, street hooligans, Brownshirts, would go to the campaign rallies of rival parties like the communists and socialists where they would wreak havoc by starting fights and causing general disorder. America's own conservative Brownshirt activity bears a striking resemblance to the events of early Nazi Germany. Then Texas Governor Bush's campaign sent paid campaign staffers and office staffers of conservative congressmen from D.C. to "rallies" at vote counting facilities in Florida to pose as ordinary Floridians who were attempting to prevent alleged "election fraud." In reality, they only wanted to disenfranchise those Floridians whose votes were not counted in the original tally. In 2004, conservative Brownshirts appeared at numerous John Kerry public presidential rallies attempting to shout the candidate down for the television cameras while the Bush-Cheney campaign held closed (for only the party faithful and donors) campaign rallies and events so that the Kerry campaign could not respond in kind.

However, rival politicians are not the only persons affected as a consequence of Bush's insidious anti-free speech/expression message. Ordinary citizens have fallen victim to this as well. A woman from Woodland, Washington was kicked off of a Southwest Airlines flight for wearing a T-shirt that was critical of President Bush, Secretary of State Condoleezza Rice, and Vice President Dick Cheney. Others have been arrested on trumped up charges of disturbing the peace for everything from wearing T-shirts to booing while attending Bush few public campaign events.

The Administration's anti-speech/expression activities took on new meaning in the aftermath of the September 11, 2001 attacks. White House Press Secretary Ari Fleischer, paraphrasing, warned Americans that they better watch what they say when addressing Bill Maher's statement that the 9/11 terrorists were not cowards. Fleisher's statement implies that because the country had just been attacked the government could somehow suspend the First Amendment. With the war in Afghanistan well underway and the Bush Administration taking concerted and certain action to get congressional authorization to invade Iraq, the Bush Administration began infiltrating peace groups and tracking the organizations' electronic communications that were seen as a threat to advancing the regime's war planning for invading Iraq as pointed out in Michael Moore's Fahrenheit 911 where he pointed out that even local law enforcement officials were taking up Bushes illegal cause. This illustrates that the government did not use the unconstitutional Patriot Act for the purposes they initially claimed it would be limited to; tracking terrorists. This also illustrates clearly President Bush's plan to expand government power at the expense of the people's liberty (i.e. free speech and association).

These assaults on liberty are just the tip of the iceberg in the Bush Administration's attempt to expand presidential power at the expense of the people's liberty. With the two wars ongoing and the threat of Al Qaeda seemingly unpredictable, Bush claimed unprecedented powers under the Commander-in-Chief clause of the Constitution on the grounds that constitutional limitations imposed by the Bill of Rights must give way to protect the homeland from terrorists, some of which were rejected by the Supreme Court of the United States, the co-equal and third branch of government, in Rasul v. Bush, 542 U.S. 466 (2004) and Hamdi v. Rumsfeld, 542 U.S. 507 (2004). Notwithstanding the fact that this sounds extremely similar to Hitler's justifications for invading Czechoslovakia and Poland, the limitations on governmental authority that the Founding Fathers enshrined in our Constitution were intended to protect the people from the government becoming tyrannical and arbitrary (i.e. government acting beyond its constitutional authority) in their exercise of the limited powers the people granted it.

Conservatives' penchant toward tyranny is not new. From the early days of the republic, conservatives have tried to find ways to usurp constitutional limitations on governmental authority over the people. Federalist President John Adams and the Federalist-controlled Congress passed the Alien and Seditions Act of 1798 with the intended goal of deporting foreign citizens believed to be a "threat" (i.e. speaking ill of government officials) to the United States as well as criminally penalizing Americans who engaged in criticism of the government with prison sentences and fines. The liberals, led by James Madison and Thomas Jefferson, were astonished at how quickly the government had attempted to undermine the newly enshrined constitutional protections of the Bill of Rights (adopted 1791). While these laws were eventually repealed with the election of Thomas Jefferson as president and his Democratic-Republican party[43] winning control of Congress in the election of 1800, this was not the last time that conservatives attempted to undermine our Constitution.

American history is littered with presidents' attempts to usurp constitutional limitations on their power by claiming expansive executive powers contrary to the Bill of Rights and the principles of separation of powers. President Abraham Lincoln, without congressional authorization, suspended the writ of habeas corpus giving federal authorities free reign to

---

[43] This party was the precursor of the modern Democratic party that arose under President Andrew Jackson.

detain suspected Confederate sympathizers and spies without charges or an opportunity to challenge their detention. Under a 1918 Sedition law, President Woodrow Wilson tried to restrict free speech by criminally prosecuting the government's detractors (critics of officials and the military) like Eugene V. Debs who received 10 year prison sentences repeating the mistake that led to the end of the Federalist Party. President Franklin D. Roosevelt placed tens of thousands of Japanese Americans into concentration camps and allowed their personal and real property to be taken by other private citizens without due process of law.[44] President Richard M. Nixon authorized warrantless surveillance, electronic and otherwise, of Americans he believed to be opposed to his administration. Finally, President Ronald W. Reagan authorized the selling of weapons to the militant, anti-American Iranian regime and the use of the funds to support the Nicaraguan Contras who were fighting a civil war against the popular, leftist Sandinista government despite Congress having passed legislation prohibiting such activity. There is only one example in American history in which a president was turned back in his assertion of expanded Commander-in-Chief powers; President Harry Truman, until stopped by the Supreme Court of the United States, attempted to nationalize the steel industry during a period of labor unrest to prevent a steel shortage during the Korean War. These are just a few of the examples of presidents violating constitutional and statutory limitations to their authority.

Unlike any other presidential administration, the conservative Bush Administration has attempted to usurp the constitutional safeguards that shield the people from arbitrary and tyrannical rule more than any other administration in American history. In fact, in May of 1999 then presidential candidate George W. Bush stated that "[t]here ought to be limits to freedom" when responding to criticism that he had received.[45] This statement is very insightful of what the future President Bush's approach toward civil liberties would be. For example, Bush's view point on the importance of the American public having access to information from a free press has been resoundingly unenthusiastic as the administration has been one of the most secretive in American history. This has been especially true as it relates to the American media televising images of the coffins of America's war dead returning home.

In the United Kingdom, dead soldiers' remains are repatriated from

---

[44] Surprisingly the government did not intern Japanese Americans of Hawaii despite there being a much higher concentration of them there than on the mainland.

[45] Terry M. Neal, "Satirical Web Site Poses Political Test Facing Legal Action From Bush, Creator Cites U.S. Tradition of Parody," *Washington Post*, November 29, 1999, accessed November 24, 2013, http://www.washingtonpost.com/wp-srv/WPcap/1999-11/29/002r-112999-idx.html.

Iraq in solemn ceremonies with the media present to carry the message of human sacrifice to the public and allow all Britons to, if they choose, observe the return of their soldiers and pay their respects. British Prime Minister Tony Blair was not absolutely popular with his countrymen for his decision to go to war in Iraq but he still believed it necessary for the media to have access to, and coverage of, the repatriation of Britain's war dead because he understood that the people have a right to the information, nay, a right to know the true costs of war. Even Canada's Conservative Prime Minister Stephen Harper allowed the media to cover the placement of dead Canadian troops in aircraft for repatriation from Afghanistan in 2006.

However, President Bush remains steadfast in his opposition because he claims that it would violate the privacy of the family members of the dead as well as expose them to more pain. Seeing a flag-draped coffin does not reveal the identity of the dead soldiers. This excuse is merely the Bush Administration attempt to hide the real reason. The real reason the Bush Administration is opposed to Americans viewing the return of the coffins relates to the Vietnam War. In the 1960s, as more and more coffins returned to Dover Air Force Base in Delaware, Americans began to see the true cost of war. Hearing the numbers of war dead is not the same as seeing a coffin that you know contains the lifeless body of some young American who died fighting a war cooked up by conservatives in Washington, D.C. for the sole purpose of divesting Iraqis of their oil reserves and placing it in the hands of American and European oil corporations. Seeing these coffins we would know that a young American will not be able to see his/her family again or be able to pursue their remaining hopes and dreams. Bush is hoping that by hiding pictures of this grisly reality Americans will not clue in to what war really is and what it does to humanity. If Americans were to realize this, their support for his ill-advised adventure in Iraq and other warmongering policies would dwindle and dry up just as it did during the Vietnam War.

If the media of a constitutional monarchy, where the Queen holds the sovereignty, has the right to film and photograph the return of the nation's war dead's coffins, the media of this republic, where sovereignty lies with the people, have the same right. Bush Administration officials know that an informed public is a dangerous public to government that does not meet the people's expectations. Conservatives, like Bush, also realize that access to reliable information is also dangerous to their attempts to manipulate the masses. So limiting the information available to the public is the best way for Bush and his conservative zealots to continue to recklessly wield American power in the world. While the photographing and filming of coffins may seem minor, that is merely the beginning when it comes to the Bush Administration's assault on the free press.

Helen Thomas, a longtime member of the White House press

corps, jumped out of the frying pan into the fire when she asked several critical questions of President Bush and Press Secretary Ari Fleischer during several press conferences. Thomas, who had questioned presidents and their press secretaries since the Kennedy Administration, was famously ignored during a White House Press Conference in March 2003 by President George W. Bush. The Bush Administration also stripped her of the customary "Thank you, Mr. President" that she delivered at the end of every presidential press conference. The goal of this act was to intimidate members of the White House press corps into not asking the president uncomfortable questions. Rather than showing signs of press solidarity by boycotting future press conferences, the "liberal media" failed to come to Helen's defense or the defense of the concept of a free press when they yielded to Ari Fleischer's insistence on scripting questions for Bush. If the "liberal media" had drawn the line in the sand at that very moment perhaps the Bush Administration's tactics for silencing the press for asking the hard questions would have fallen flat but they did not and the freedom of the press in this country suffered as a result and emboldened the president to take his anti-free press stance offshore.

In 2005, a British civil servant revealed details contained in a secret government memorandum to *The Daily Mirror* that outlined a conversation between British Prime Minister Tony Blair and President Bush at the White House about bombing Al-Jazeera, the satellite news agency located in Doha, Qatar.[46] Apparently, Prime Minister Blair convinced Bush that it would be a bad idea. Al-Jazeera is the Arab world's only independent, non-state-controlled media source. During an April 16, 2004, meeting between the two leaders, according to the secret memorandum, Bush raised the issue of bombing Al-Jazeera because the Arab satellite news agency fuels anti-American attitudes in the region.

Al-Jazeera is accused of fanning the flames of anti-Americanism by airing footage of apartment buildings and homes hit by errant American missiles and bombs, Al Qaeda video and audio statements, as well as being a mouthpiece for former Iraqi President Saddam Hussein during the invasion including providing intelligence to the regime of U.S. troop movements. In fact, U.S. Secretary of Defense Donald Rumsfeld accused Al-Jazeera of hurting the U.S. effort to bring regime change to Iraq and the rest of the Middle East by airing footage intended to demonize U.S. forces justifying U.S. attacks on the news agency.

There is already evidence that the Bush Administration has targeted Al-Jazeera's offices and reporters. In November 2002, a U.S. missile

---

[46] See Robert Barr, "Did Blair persuade Bush not to bomb Al-Jazeera?", *The Seattle Times,* November 22, 2005, accessed December 1, 2005, http://seattletimes.nwsource.com.

destroyed an unoccupied Al-Jazeera office in Kabul, Afghanistan that the administration believed was a terrorist site not a news agency. The Bush Administration claimed to have mistakenly bombed Al-Jazeera's Baghdad office in April 2003 killing a journalist who occupied the office at the time. Essentially, the Bush Administration's position is simply that if you report unflattering stories about the Bush Administration's conduct of the Iraq and/or Afghanistan war then we revoke your right to engage in the practice of the freedom of the press and, even more importantly, revoke your right to live.

There is no doubt that the people of the Arab world viewing footage of the aftermath of U.S. bombs and missiles hitting the wrong target and harming civilians is negative. However, media is not intended to only report positive stories to the liking of governments otherwise it would become propaganda rather than news. Part of a free press' duties is to provide information so that the people can decide what actions, if any, need to be taken against a government engaging in tyrannical or arbitrary conduct as the people exercise oversight of their government. As for Al-Jazeera reporting stories favorable to Saddam Hussein and providing intelligence to his military officials, Al-Jazeera is, and has in the past, been widely viewed as an enemy of the despotic authoritarian regimes of the Middle East including the late Saddam Hussein. This news organization's reporters have been threatened or jailed from Syria to Iran for trying to bring the truth to the people in hopes that the people will be able to empower themselves to defeat the despots who control their societies.

Instead of communicating to the Arab world the importance of pluralism and liberty, Bush has communicated, through his actions, that he is no different from Saddam Hussein; that is to say Bush actions indicate a desire to suppress viewpoints that differ from his own despite Bush making speeches at nearly every public appearance where he extols the importance of bringing freedom to the Iraqi people including a free press. However, Bush's threat to destroy Al-Jazeera has had exactly the opposite effect on the region and, perhaps, irreparably injured America's reputation among Arabs. The people of the Middle East see that Bush was just as willing as their current autocratic leaders to suppress disfavored viewpoints. Instead of creating an appeal for plural, liberal, democratic societies, Bush has convinced many that America's ideals and principles are nothing but rhetoric and that America really is a greedy imperial power looking to expand its economic control over the whole of the Middle East's petroleum reserves. If this viewpoint is left unchecked, the war in Iraq, based on the Bush Administrations' own justifications (i.e. liberty and democracy), would have been for nothing. While this Al-Jazeera bombing plot proves to be exceptionally heinous, this would not be the only or the most egregious of President Bush's attempts to undermine the concept of civil liberties. In the days following the destruction of the World Trade Center, Bush would declare the constitutional principle barring "unreasonable searches and seizures" null and void.

The much of the public and the Congress were in a state of shock and confusion about how to respond to the villainous actions of Al Qaeda. However, the conservatives in charge of Congress knew exactly how to respond to this infamously historic event; increase the government's power, particularly that of the president, and reduce those pesky civil liberties to dead letters that would be mere footnotes in history. The beginning, Congress adopted and the president signed the USA PATRIOT Act. The Patriot Act was adopted in the immediate weeks following the destruction of the World Trade Center. The faux panacea to America's terror problem contained numerous provisions but here we will review two of the most constitutionally questionable provisions. First, the Patriot Act allowed the Bush Administration to obtain, through the issuance of a National Security Letter (NSL), personal records (library, medical, telephone, and consumer transactions) and prevent NSL recipients from even disclosing that they had received such a letter thereby preventing recipients from challenging the validity of the governmental order to turn over information and items.[47] These NSLs are essentially warrantless searches and seizures of private information and records; warrantless searches are per se unconstitutional under the Fourth Amendment because the government is required to obtain a warrant that is supported by probable cause before it may search and seize people or their property with a few limited exceptions.

Secondly, the Patriot Act also expanded the application of the Foreign Intelligence Surveillance Act (FISA) of 1978 to U.S. citizens. FISA was originally created to allow for domestic surveillance of foreign nationals and diplomats suspected of being spies operating within the United States. Under FISA, a secret panel of federal judges would review government requests for warrants to secretly search and seize foreign officials and their property if they were suspected of being spies. FISA even has an emergency provision that allows the government to engage in surveillance of these individuals for up to 72 hours before reporting any of the actions to the FISA court for its review. Under a FISA warrant the government could engage in electronic surveillance of persons as well as search and seize property without disclosing the fact that the search and/or seizure took place. Putting aside the fact that the NSL nondisclosure provision of the Patriot Act may violate the recipient's freedom of speech rights as a prior restraint on a person's right to speak, which our constitutional

---

[47] Lara Jakes Jordan, "More FBI Privacy Violations Confirmed," *The Seattle Times*, March 6, 2008, http://seattletimes.nwsource.com/html/politics/2004261432_apsenatefbi.html.

jurisprudence disfavors, extending the application of FISA to American citizens raise many other constitutional and moral questions. One case in particular shows how the Patriot Act in general and the FISA warrants in particular can violate a person's constitutional rights when overzealous federal officials believe a person is engaging in illegal conduct without any evidence.[48]

  In 2004, Islamic right-wing terrorists decimated a train station in Madrid, Spain with bombs that killed scores of innocent Spaniards. The FBI assisted the Spanish government in investigating the attack. The FBI identified Portland attorney Brandon Mayfield as a suspect. Mayfield, a recent convert to Islam, had represented some individuals from Portland who were subsequently convicted of planning acts of terrorism in the United States and going to Pakistan to meet with members of Al Qaeda for terrorist training. The agency's fingerprint analysts believed that one of the fingerprints found on an unexploded device belonged to Mayfield despite there being no similarities between the fingerprint that was found and Mayfield's. Furthermore, Spanish law enforcement warned the FBI before they took Mayfield into custody that the fingerprint match was erroneous. However, the FBI analysts believed that Mayfield was the suspect because of his recent conversion and his ties to the convicted Portland group. After two weeks of confinement and destruction of his reputation, the FBI admitted that it had mistakenly arrested Mayfield and released him with an apology.

  Mayfield filed a civil action against the government that challenges the validity of the Patriot Act among other things. While preparing for the ensuing litigation, Mayfield and his attorney learned that the FBI had used FISA warrants to obtain wiretaps of his home and to secretly enter his home and search and seize certain items without his knowledge in the spring of 2004. In denying the government's motion to dismiss Mayfield's lawsuit, a federal district court judge in Portland ruled that the FBI needs to disclose to Mayfield the warrants and details of the search and seizure (i.e. what items were seized during the secret search of Mayfield's home). Essentially the court recognized that the Constitution does not give government unfettered access to persons and/or their property simply because the government believes the person is a terrorist except where there are facts that support a reasonable belief that the person is or has engaged in criminal conduct (i.e. terrorist activity or planning). In his case,

---

[48] The constitutional principle of "innocent until proven guilty" also took a major beating during this instance. This principle has its origins in the English common law and was adopted by the drafters of our Constitution as a way to counter the great authority that is at the disposal of government authorities (e.g. law enforcement) vis a vis the individual.

there was no probable cause to believe that Mayfield engaged in terrorist acts. In fact, the federal judge found that the Patriot Acts amendments to FISA were unconstitutional.[49]

Bush and his conservative cronies support the Patriot Act on the grounds that terrorists will be able to enter our country and destroy our way of life if we do not roll back some of our constitutional civil liberties that hinder the government's ability to provide security to Americans. This line of thinking is extremely flawed because it does not recognize the obvious. By rolling back our constitutional protections to allow for the government to intrude further into our lives, the terrorists have already destroyed our way of life. Americans need to be brave and accept that government cannot provide perfect protection from the threats posed by Al Qaeda and other terrorist organizations whether they are foreign or domestic and demand that the government provide security within and in compliance with our Constitution's limitations on its authority to interfere in our lives. If we do not take this small step as a society, we will have abandoned our reverence for the rule of law and liberty and submitted ourselves over to tyranny and arbitrary exercises of power.

While Congress' extension of dubious powers under the Patriot Act are damaging enough to our Constitution, conservative President Bush has unilaterally asserted that he has expansive powers under the Commander-in-Chief clause of the Constitution that allow the president to "protect" the United States despite the Constitution's prohibition of some activities. One of the most dangerous of these extensions of power is the right to detain any person suspected of being a terrorist <u>indefinitely</u>, U.S. citizen or not. Our Constitution requires that whenever the government, federal or state, detains someone suspected of engaging in unlawful conduct the accused person be given an opportunity to challenge his detention.[50] This usually occurs when the accused person receives a public and speedy trial before an impartial jury of his/her peers, the right to confront the witnesses against him/her, the right to counsel, and the right to challenge the validity of the evidence against him/her. In the alternative, persons who believe they have been unlawfully detained by the government may also file petitions for writs of habeas corpus when they have no other means to challenge said detention except where Congress has suspended the great writ.

The U.S. government has captured numerous American citizens and foreign nationals who are suspected of being members of Al Qaeda or other terrorist organizations. These individuals are being held at various

---

[49] <u>Mayfield et al. v. USA</u>, 04-1427-AA p. 14.

[50] In addition, several treaties to which the United States is a signatory party to declare the rights of prisoners of war (Taliban soldiers).

locations around the world with many foreign nationals being confined at Guantanamo Bay Naval Base in Cuba. The Americans who have been captured have been held in U.S. military custody at military installations in the United States. The Supreme Court of the United States has decided several cases adversely in regards to Bush's assertions that he can arbitrarily detain individuals during the continuation of his war on terrorism.

In Rasul v. Bush, the Court ruled that foreign nationals held at Guantanamo Bay Naval Base could have access to U.S. courts for the purpose of challenging their classifications as enemy combatants using the federal habeas corpus statute based on the fact that the base is U.S. territory and detainees need a way of challenging alleged erroneous detentions. In Hamdi v. Rumsfeld, the Court, in a plurality opinion, stated that a U.S. citizen had a right to some form of procedural due process as required by the Constitution because there was no way to tell how long the war on terror would last and the Constitution abhors lifelong detentions without any way of challenging that detention. The Court failed to clarify what process was due to Hamdi and other detainees. In fact, in Associate Justice Sandra Day O'Connor's plurality opinion she makes an allusion that Bush's military tribunals may provide the necessary process for the detainees. Nevertheless, the Court has made it clear to administration officials that the President of the United States does not possess the authority to detain any person, U.S. citizen or not, indefinitely without providing a way for that person to challenge his detention or his classification as an enemy combatant. Even more recently, the Court has declared President Bush's military tribunals unconstitutional as they have not been authorized by Congress and the President does not have the unilateral authority to create such military tribunals.[51]

---

[51] Hamdan v. Rumsfeld, 548 U.S. 557 (2006). Conservatives often subscribe to the view that foreign nationals should not be granted protection under our constitution because they are not U.S. citizens and that U.S. citizens who fight against the United States should not receive protection under the Constitution that they sought to destroy. Adherence to our Constitution is not optional and if we were to follow the reasoning of conservatives the terrorists would have won by getting us to abandon our fundamental legal principles that separate us from the rest of the world. Additionally, the Founding Fathers drafted the Constitution and carefully made distinctions between "citizens" and "persons" when discussing various rights and privileges. For example, when talking about who may become president, senators, and representatives the Constitution uses the requirement of citizenship. However, when talking about the limitations on governmental authority as it relates to individuals, such as the Fourth Amendment, the Constitution uses the word "persons." The distinction was intended to indicate that while some things were reserved for citizens only, others were available to all who resided within the United States regardless of citizenship status.

These cases illustrate that all persons, citizens and non-citizens alike, within the United States jurisdiction, have a constitutional due process right to challenge their detention as enemy combatants as well as a right to challenge their detention in the federal courts under the federal habeas corpus statute. The right to detain anybody for any reason and for an indefinite period of time is not the only unilateral expansion of presidential authority undertaken by Fuhrer Bush. He has also claimed that his commander-in-chief powers allow him to engage in electronic surveillance on American soil without constitutional and/or statutory authorization.

Bush claims that, in the interest of detecting sleeper terrorist cells in the United States, it was necessary to allow the National Security Agency to listen in on any Americans phone calls and read any Americans email, text messages, and other electronic communications without a warrant at any time. The news of the program's existence was broken by the New York Times in December 2005. Bush specifically claimed that he created the NSA domestic spying program in response to two of the 9-11 terrorists, Nawaf al Hazmi and Khalid al-Mihdhar, who crashed into the Pentagon, having made several telephone calls to a suspected terrorist safe house in Yemen while in San Diego. Bush claims that the two September 11 terrorists would have been apprehended or the plot discovered had U.S. intelligence agencies been able to review electronic communications (i.e. telephone and email). Additionally, Bush asserts that FISA is too slow in responding to terrorist threats so as commander-in-chief he has the authority to unilaterally ignore that law.

Notwithstanding Bush's spy program's violation of the Constitution, when his administration created the electronic spying program it violated the Patriot Act's procedures; legislation the administration specifically requested Congress pass for the purpose of combating international terrorism. The legally questionable Patriot Act explicitly allowed the executive branch to obtain FISA secret warrants in order to fight terrorism domestically. In addition, FISA allows government officials to engage in warrantless electronic surveillance of Americans in emergencies for a period of up to 72 hours before the U.S. Attorney General is required to notify the FISA court and seek a warrant. This is completely inconsistent with President Bush's assertion that FISA was too slow in granting authorization for those reviews.

The real problem for American intelligence, according to Bush's own 9-11 Commission's report, was a communication breakdown between those agencies that routinely gather information about terrorist threats, in particular the FBI and the NSA.[52] According to the report, the CIA did not place Nawaf al Hazmi, one of the 9/11 hijackers, on the terrorist watch list

---

[52] 9/11 Commission Report, p. 87-88.

or notify the FBI of his presence in the United States in 2000.[53] Additionally, two hijackers, including Hazmi, had been linked to intercepted telephone calls between a Yemen safe house, previously linked to the 1998 and 2000 bombings of the U.S. embassies and the U.S.S. Cole, and the two terrorists' San Diego apartment but the NSA failed to share that information with the FBI.[54] These failures of the intelligence community to talk to one another and many others like it illustrate the fact that the government does not need more power to spy on Americans as Bush suggests; instead, the government should use what it currently has in its possession and do its job of providing security within the confines of the Constitution of the United States.

So, Bush's claim that he did not seek a FISA warrant to create the domestic electronic surveillance program because FISA is too slow for responding to terrorist threats are not supported by the facts. Even more damning to administration's claims was then Attorney General Alberto Gonzalez's failure to provide a response when asked what additional tools the government needed to assist in the fight against international terrorism in a congressional hearing. The dishonesty, immorality, and lack of human decency of the Bush Administration clearly demonstrate that our civil liberties are in jeopardy but we stand to lose something else; we stand to lose our standing in the world as a beacon of justice and fairness.

While our Constitution may require that we extend constitutional protections (i.e. procedural due process) to all persons within the United States jurisdiction, including non-citizens like terror suspects, there is an even better reason why we, as Americans, should want to extend these constitutional rights to these individuals in criminal proceedings before our civilian courts. The world would see that our system of justice works because it will protect the interests of the accused person while, at the same time, ensuring that those who are guilty of engaging in criminal conduct are punished appropriately for those acts. The Pacific Northwest provides the perfect example of how our judiciary can successfully and fairly deal with terror suspects while protecting their civil rights, our national security, and, most importantly, our identity as expressed in our constitutionally protected liberties.

On December 16, 1999, United States border officials detained Algerian-born Ahmed Ressam at the port of entry in Port Angeles, Washington when he departed a ferry from Victoria, British Columbia, Canada, with bomb making materials. Federal law enforcement officials uncovered Ressam's plot to bomb the Los Angeles International Airport on

---

[53] 9/11 Commission Report, p. 355.
[54] Josh Meyer, "Officials poke holes in Bush's case for wiretaps," *The Seattle Times (Los Angeles Times)*, December 22, 2005, http://www.seattletimes.com.

the eve of the millennium. In April 2001, a federal jury convicted Ressam of several offenses but it would not be until July 2005 when Ressam learned what his sentence would be because the court permitted federal law enforcement officials to question Ressam with the goal of learning valuable information about other terror plots and suspected terrorists. At his sentencing, Ressam learned that he would spend twenty-two years in federal prison for his actions which took into account his cooperation with federal law enforcement officials by providing valuable information about other terror suspects and plots. While the facts surrounding Ahmed Ressam's trial and conviction are important, the statement made by Ressam's sentencing judge are even more important to illustrate that our justice system can effectively deal with terror suspects despite President George W. Bush's statements to the contrary.

While handing down Ressam's sentence, U.S. District Court Chief Judge, The Honorable John Coughenour, a Reagan appointee, spoke out against the Bush Administration's tactics in dealing with suspected Al Qaeda terrorists. Chief Judge Coughenour stated

> The message I would hope to convey in today's sentencing is two-fold: First, that we have the resolve in this country to deal with the subject of terrorism and people who engage in it should be prepared to sacrifice a major portion of their life in confinement.

> Secondly, though, I would like to convey the message that our system works. We did not need to use a secret military tribunal, or detain the defendant indefinitely as an enemy combatant, or deny him the right to counsel, or invoke any proceedings beyond those guaranteed by or contrary to the United States Constitution.

> I would suggest that the message to the world from today's sentencing is that our courts have not abandoned our commitment to the ideals that set our nation apart. We can deal with the threats to our national security without denying the accused fundamental constitutional protections.

> Despite the fact that Mr. Ressam is not an American citizen and despite the fact that he entered this country intent upon killing American citizens, he received

an effective, vigorous defense, and the opportunity to have his guilt or innocence determined by a jury of 12 ordinary citizens.

Most importantly, all of this occurred in the sunlight of a public trial. There were no secret proceedings, no indefinite detention, no denial of counsel.

The tragedy of September 11th shook our sense of security and made us realize that we, too, are vulnerable to acts of terrorism. Unfortunately, some believe that this threat renders our Constitution obsolete. This is a Constitution for which men and women have died and continue to die and which has made us a model among nations. If that view is allowed to prevail, the terrorists will have won.

It is my sworn duty, and as long as there is breath in my body I'll perform it, to support and defend the Constitution of the United States.

We will be in recess.[55]

Ressam's trial, conviction, and sentencing should signal clearly to Bush Administration officials and his conservative cohorts that the American justice system is capable of dealing with these individuals in such a way that on the one hand they will face justice for their evil conduct and national security is protected while on the other hand their civil liberties and rights are protected. This has the additional effect of protecting our identity as Americans. Ressam's trial and conviction completely contradicts the Bush Administration's claim that in order to fight an effective war on terror he needs the unfettered ability to detain terror suspects indefinitely, without criminal charges, and without outside contact; all of these things are violations of our Constitution.

Not only do Bush's indefinite detentions violate the Constitution but they also violate long-established principles of international law. Bush refuses to recognize Taliban fighters' rights as prisoners of war because they did not have on military uniforms and denies fair trials to accused international criminals that are suspected members of Al Qaeda on the

---

[55] Chief Judge John Coughenour, <u>U.S. v. Ressam Transcript</u>, July 27, 2005.

grounds that he needs to determine what information they know as well as not give terror suspects a stage from which to spread their message or to give coded orders that might set in motion a terror attack on United States' interests abroad or at home.[56] However, the U.S. government admittedly gained extensive amounts of intelligence from discussions with Ahmed Ressam after he was convicted and before his sentencing. In fact, that is why his sentencing was delayed so that U.S. government officials could question the convicted Algerian terrorist. He provided U.S. intelligence officials with the names of alleged terror suspects and associates as well as terror plots.

Let us not forget that the U.S. government just recently tried and convicted Zacarias Moussaoui who was initially believed to be the twentieth hijacker. However, it has since been proven that he had no role in the September 11, 2001, plot but was merely a wannabe rejected by Al Qaeda who yelled anti-American slogans day-in and day-out in court yet no terrorist sleepers were activated and his statements sounded as if they were coming from a man suffering from mental illness rather than a well-trained purveyor of terror. Indefinite detentions are not the only violations of domestic and international law served up by the Bush Administration.

The Bush Administration has come under fire for allegedly secretly transporting terror suspects on flights through European airports, snatching alleged terrorists off of the streets, and running secret prisons in Eastern European countries to detain alleged terrorists. This program is known as Extraordinary Rendition. The Council of Europe, a human rights organization to which 46 European nations belong, conducted investigations into these allegations to determine if the United States violated any European human rights laws. While the Bush Administration has confirmed the existence of an alleged small number of high value prisoners, the circumstantial evidence that European investigators have encountered suggests a substantial number of detainees held in numerous black sites.

In fact, a 72 page Council of Europe report implicated Bosnia, Cyprus, Germany, Greece, Ireland, Italy, Macedonia, Poland, Portugal, Romania, Spain, Sweden, Turkey, and the United Kingdom as having cooperated with the CIA's secret flights carrying alleged terrorists who were abducted and detained in violation of international law.[57] Additionally,

---

[56] Remember, international law sets rules for handling both prisoners of war (persons engaged in combat on behalf of another state) and unlawful combatants (persons engaged in combat as mercenaries as well as terrorists). Prisoners of war should be protected under the Geneva Conventions, a set of treaties to which the United States is a signatory state, and unlawful combatants should be treated as criminals under the municipal (domestic) law of the country that they are violating.
[57] Dick Marty, *Secret Detentions and Illegal transfers of detainees involving Council of Europe*

Poland and Romania are suspected of allowing the CIA to run secret prisons based on evidence gathered by the Rapporteur Dick Marty. "A parallel investigation by the European Parliament has said data show there have been more than 1,000 CIA flights stopping on European territory since the Sept. 11, 2001, attacks."[58] Despite efforts to promote democracy and foster openness in newly independent Eastern Europe, the Bush Administration set the efforts back by encouraging Eastern European governments to engage in secret activities that violate the human and civil rights of many people. At this point, a clear pattern has emerged that demonstrates that conservatives do not and will not honor the promise of the American Constitution and of international conventions.

While the Constitution does not apply to other governments, it should inform and influence the decisions of American presidential administrations when engaging in international diplomacy. Bush's willingness to violate the rights of Americans and non-Americans alike should offend and anger any decent red-blooded American. His actions will render our constitutional liberties a dead letter. Especially if Americans continue to accept his assertions that security should always take precedent over liberty. This administration has sought to gain our acquiescence through our fear. Bush uses our fear to convince us that there is a terrorist lurking around every corner by raising and lowering the terror alert from yellow to orange and back and forth. This acquiescence can only have the effect of obliterating our Constitution. We must stand and defend these liberties if they are to survive in the face of this conservative, some would say fascist, onslaught.

While conservatives are often up-in-arms over people burning the flag, they say nary a word to defend our constitutional liberties that are being dismantled before our very eyes. When I joined the United States Navy so many years ago, my oath was not to protect and defend the flag. My oath was to protect and defend the Constitution of the United States of America and I challenge those faux Americans, the conservatives, to stand in defense of the liberty that our Constitution protects. Flags are important symbols but constitutional liberties are even more important as they limit our government's authority in this republic and they signify who we are as a people. These liberties are what ensure that the people remain sovereign over the government that serves them. Without these liberties, the tyranny feared by Thomas Jefferson and James Madison would surely result and America would be a shell of what she was originally intended to be; a place

---

member states: second report, Committee on Legal Affairs and Human Rights, June 7, 2007,

[58] Jan Sliva, , "Probe of CIA Prisons Implicates EU Nations," *Tacoma News Tribune (Associated Press)*, June 7, 2006.

where the people use their sovereignty to elect the individuals who govern in their stead with as little interference as possible in the people's ability to live their lives according to their own terms and associating with other individuals as they see fit.

Tyranny often rears its ugly head when those in power begin to question the patriotism of those who do not agree with them. It shows itself when those in power begin to monitor the communications of their political opponents. It shows itself when average citizens are terminated from jobs for their dissent from the majority perspective. In this republic, the civil liberties enshrined in our Constitution are intended to protect the right of dissenters to freely speak without threat from the government. Bush and his conservative cronies' attack on America's fundamental principles have had a spillover effect in international affairs that has harmed America's world standing and advanced the cause of authoritarianism and corporate imperialism.

CHAPTER 4: U.S. CONSERVATIVE FOREIGN POLICY: FROM ISOLATION TO WORLD DOMINATION

Conservatives often attack liberals by saying that liberals want to understand terrorists not fight them. As a liberal, I would agree with that statement with this qualification. Most liberals believe that in order to fight terrorism you need to, in conjunction with a vigilant and persistent law enforcement effort, understand the reasons for so many young Muslims joining groups that want to destroy the West. There is obviously something about American foreign policy that drives young, oftentimes educated, people to want to kill themselves in bombings and firefights, which I will return to later.

The conservative response is to call for war exclusive of an examination of the reasons for Hamas, Hezbollah, and Al Qaeda successfully recruiting thousands of young people. I liken the conservative's response to visiting a physician for a diagnosis and treatment plan. If your physician informs you that your liver is showing signs of damage and the physician informs you that you can no longer drink alcohol yet you continue to drink despite the ominous warning. By ignoring the problem, you expedite your own demise because you refuse to acknowledge the elephant in the room. Conservatives believe that you can quickly solve all problems by blowing someone or something up (use of violence is a common occurrence in fascist political movements).

Initially, the conservative Bush Administration led the American people to believe that its war on terror would be won in short order by capturing or killing Al Qaeda's leadership, which would prevent successful terrorist attacks in the future. This has been far from the truth. Despite the Bush Administration taking 9-11 mastermind Khalid Sheikh Muhammad into custody, Al Qaeda and its affiliates still managed to bomb a Madrid train station and several London buses and subway trains. After killing thousands of people, on both sides, and destroying countless homes and businesses in Afghanistan, Osama bin Laden and his lieutenants continue to release audio and video statements about the holy war they are waging to rally their supporters. Even more importantly, they recruit innumerable young disaffected Muslims regardless of racial or ethnic differences to join their cause who see the video footage of dead and dying Muslims in the aftermath of U.S. bombings as a sign of the United States disregard for Muslim lives. Thus, the conservative's approach to dealing with terrorism merely exacerbates the problem making the world a less secure place and swells the ranks of terror organizations.

Much of the blame for the American public's willingness to accept the Bush Administration's assertions that the war in Afghanistan and Iraq would end quickly is related to the American people's naiveté about the resiliency and patients of terrorists who truly believe in their cause and their willingness to die in their terrorist/paramilitary operations. Additionally, the Bush Administration exacerbated and played off of this naiveté by promoting an environment of fear where Americans were advised to purchase duct tape and plastic wrap to protect them in their homes from supposed terror attacks involving biological/chemical agents while national security officials played with the newly created color-coded terrorist threat level system (fear meter) to create panic as needed by the administration and then Attorney General John Ashcroft told Americans that they should report any suspicious activity of their neighbors to the TIPS program in the U.S. Department of Justice because their neighbors may be sleeper terrorist cells waiting for official orders to launch their attacks. Under these conditions the American people were willing to do anything the Bush Administration wanted. However, the Bush Administration made a miscalculation.

Americans are not as persistent as those terrorists who are willing to engage in decade-after-decade of military combat and covert terror operations. For most Americans, wars are fought on distant battlefields with weapons that are like video games without any threat of direct enemy attacks on continental U.S. soil at least since the War of 1812.[59] On the other hand, Europeans know firsthand that terrorism can last for decades and costs thousands of lives; whether you are talking about the Algerian nationalist carrying out bombings in France, the Irish Republican Army (IRA) launching missions on the streets of London that kill scores of individuals, Basque separatists ETA assassinating government officials in Spain, or November 17 attacking Greek officials and foreign diplomats

---

[59] It is not the Mexican War because the war was largely fought on Mexican soil.

alike, Europeans have lived with the threat of terror attacks for decades and to some extent decided that they cannot stop living their lives nor give up their general freedom because of the threat of some fanatical terror group.

Israelis currently have similar experiences as it relates to terrorist attacks. In fact, the Israelis do not have an elaborate color-coded threat level system as we Americans do. Unlike Americans in the wake of the 9-11 attacks, Israelis simply go about their daily lives in an attempt to prevent the terrorists from winning the upper hand by making everyone live in fear with the understanding that the government is trying its best to foil terrorist plots to bomb malls and public transit but cannot guarantee that none will occur. Terrorists wait months or even years before they carry out one of their politico-military operations.

In fact, if America's own recent history is any indicator, Al Qaeda has never been in a hurry to carry out its "operations" against the United States. Al Qaeda is patient and they decide where the battlefield is and when it is time to engage its foe. Al Qaeda affiliates bombed the World Trade Center in 1993, Khobar Towers in 1996, U.S. Embassies in Kenya and Tanzania in 1998, the U.S.S. Cole in 2000, and the World Trade Center in 2001. These terrorists are ready to wage a long drawn out war that most Americans are not.

If Americans decide to pursue this issue following the logic of conservatives they should be prepared to sacrifice countless young American service members' lives, billions of dollars of treasure, and the threat of continued covert attacks like those catalogued above for decades because this war could go on for an inordinate amount of time.[60] Notwithstanding the fact that Americans need to be aware that terrorists are patient and that life has to continue in the face of active terror threats, in the interest of our national security and ending this quagmire sooner rather than later, America needs to know, nay understand, why these reactionaries see America as their enemy; why they hate us and why so many young Muslims are willing to die for their cause?

Of course the images of blown up buildings and battered human remains after U.S. bombing raids in Iraq and Afghanistan cause Muslims great pain and contributes to young, educated, and disaffected Muslims alike joining terrorist organizations but there is even something more damaging to the United States image in the Middle East and that is our foreign policy. For decades, the United States, Israel's chief ally, stood idly by while Israel expropriated Palestinian territory that was intended for them to form their own nation-state and the U.S. government has not accepted

---

[60] Even Ronald Reagan understood that terrorists possessed the fortitude to engage the United States in sustained terror operations that is why he pulled the U.S. Marines out of Lebanon almost immediately after the bombing of their barracks.

responsibility for supporting authoritarian regimes in the Middle East (Egypt, pre-revolutionary Iran, Jordan, and Saudi Arabia).

Without these grievances being addressed, young Muslims will continue to join terrorist organizations in droves giving men like Osama bin Laden an endless supply of holy warriors despite Bush's war on terror because terrorist leaders will have issues to rally them together. Perhaps the United States government's failure to address these issues relates to the conservatives' fear that the foreign policy skeletons in their closets will tumble out into public view implicating many high-placed conservatives in un-American activities all around the globe not to mention the fact that many elite as well as lay conservatives see it as a sign of weakness for our government to admit any wrongdoing (this is a clear sign of their lack of maturity and intellect).

One consequence of our government's past actions in the Middle East is that the real freedom fighters of the Middle East ability to advance democratic ideals and institutions are hindered in their home countries because the United States provides financial and military support for stable and predictable despots who we can buy-off rather than democratically-elected governments that may not agree with U.S. leaders' positions. For example, the United States continues to support the Saudi royal family and many other autocratic regimes of the region despite these regimes engaging in activity that stifles the growth of a free press, inhibits the growth of an independent judiciary, and prevents the people from electing legislatures in a multi-party electoral process, which foments hatred for that regime in the streets of that country. In Saudi Arabia, with no alternative outlet or leadership, much of this hatred is channeled by the hardline-conservative religious clerics who direct that hatred toward the House of Saud and the United States. If many of these societies, like Saudi Arabia, became democracies overnight, it would be extremely difficult diplomatically to deal with many of the governments that would be elected because some would consist of individuals that the United States considered terrorists who would be inflexible or unwilling to deal with the United States. Nevertheless, a free people should decide their own destiny not some foreign power that just so happens to believe that it makes the best decisions.

Additionally, the United States government also comes out on the wrong side of the Israeli-Palestinian conflict as previously mentioned. While Palestinians most certainly have to recognize Israel's right to exist, Israel recognize and negotiate the conditions of Palestinians right to return to their homes as well as stop all new, and abandon all existing, Israeli settlements in the Palestinian territories. The right of return is an extremely sensitive and controversial issue because Israelis fear being overrun by the Palestinians returning to the homes and businesses they abandoned during the Israeli-Palestinian wars. Making matters even more difficult, many of the abandoned homes and businesses are now occupied by Israeli citizens. As for the settlements, Israel is consciously allowing its citizens to build homes on Palestinian land promised to the Palestinians by UN Resolutions. Addressing these two issues in the Israeli-Palestinian conflict will have the long-term effect of making it more difficult for Hezbollah and Hamas to recruit young people to carry out terrorist acts because Palestinians will be electing their own legislative and executive officials as well as have the opportunity to develop their own economy independent of the Israeli economy.

Some would say that it would be impossible to reach an agreement with some of the Palestinian factions but there are democratic steps that can be taken to isolate those factions. For example, any new proposed treaty between Israel and the Palestinians can be put to a referendum before all Palestinians. With a majority or maybe a supermajority of 60% to approve the agreement, any agreement receives legitimacy because of its support by the Palestinian people regardless of various factions being inapposite to it. As Palestinians are able to develop an economy that allows them to raise families, have careers, and attend universities, fewer and fewer individuals will be willing to join terror organizations. The terror organization loses its luster and appeal when people can live their lives with some prospect of prosperity and freedom.

The United States government also has additional amends to make in the Middle East the least of which being apologizing to the people of Iran for supporting the Shah whose brutal regime suppressed its democratic opponents and directly led to the current right-wing theocracy that oppresses that society. While this event will be discussed in further detail later, it is this and numerous other actions taken by our government in our name that have sullied the good reputation of the American people. Many of these things took place as a result of a conservative American foreign policy consumed with fighting the Cold War.

Notwithstanding the United States' economic impact on the world, most of the world learns about the United States through the effects of its foreign policy. For much of the twentieth century, American foreign policy has largely been centered on resisting the spread of communism. With communism being one of the political ideologies from the left of the political spectrum, American foreign policy has tended to rely on right-wing schemes to address and counter communism. As a result of this reliance on a conservative-centric foreign policy, the United States government has engaged in activities that many Americans would abhor if known because they are so reprehensible and contrary to our chief ideals and principles. It is these actions that are responsible for the rest of the world holding a negative opinion of the United States.

Despite the realities of what our government does to other peoples around the world, American presidential administrations' have spoken, and continue to speak, about spreading America's fundamental principles around the world but their actions do not match their rhetoric, which makes America appear to be hypocritical. American foreign policy should promote the principles of:

- Open public debate without regard to the subject matter and the ability for numerous and varying opinions to be expressed including dissenting opinions (plural)
- Liberty for all persons to pursue their full potential and goals with as little governmental interference as possible (liberal) regardless of religious, racial, ethnic or gender differences
- The people elect those who govern them in a fair multiparty electoral process (democratic)
- Ultimate authority over the government resides in the people not a single person or group of persons (republic)

Very few American presidents have actually founded foreign policy programs based on these fundamental American principles. Most presidents simply paid lip service to them while engaging in actions contrary to these principles. While the lack of ethnic diversity in the nation's foreign policy establishment is certainly a reason for American foreign policy being ineffective as former Secretary of State Colin Powell found when he took the post at Foggy Bottom, the chief reason is that presidential foreign policy agendas ignore the core principles upon which our nation was founded.

As previously mentioned, American presidents saw the spread of communism as the chief issue of the twentieth century and, in particular, dealing with its leading purveyor the Union of Soviet Socialist Republics (the Soviet Union) founded by Vladimir Lenin. The Soviet Union threatened to spread communism to every continent of the world by creating laborer and peasant uprisings against the landed gentry and the merchant class who were considered the bourgeois in hopes of destroying capitalism. Through the uprisings, the Soviets hoped to put the principles of Communism into practice. The five principles of Karl Marx's Communist ideology included (1) universal education, (2) no private property, (3) universal healthcare, (4) state ownership of the means of production, and (5) state ownership of the means of communication. In many instances, the United States fight against the spread of Communism resulted in the repression and death of many innocent civilians around the world by the supporters of the U.S.S.R. and the United States.

America's activities in the developing world often meant that the right of self-determination of the local populace were ignored for the expediency of engaging the conservative philosophy of Realpolitik. For Henry Kissinger this meant accepting the world as it currently was even if it meant the U.S. providing economic and military assistance to dictators and murderers like the Somoza regime and Pinochet's reign of death as opposed to operating under the idealistic (as Kissinger and his ilk saw it) approach of advancing our fundamental principles. In other words, Kissinger did not believe that promoting our fundamental principles (i.e. pluralism, democracy, liberty, and popular sovereignty) were all that important but that, in the interest of stopping the stalking specter of Communism (the ends), the U.S. government should engage, and where necessary, embrace dictators and murderers (the means) despite them being inapposite of what America stands for. Notwithstanding the fact that conservatives do not want to promote so-called idealistic principles because they see very little value in America's founding principles, there is a huge flaw in their position about the importance of the idealistic principles of America's Framers.

The flaw in Mr. Kissinger's view of foreign policy is that promoting idealism has been hugely successful in the international context. In the aftermath of World War II, with Europe lying under a cloud of debris and morass brought about by right-wing psychopath Hitler, the United States proposed the Marshall Plan to revitalize Europe, which prevented Western Europe from falling into a spiral of chaos, poverty, and despotism by providing about $13 billion in economic and technical assistance.[61] Western Europe developed thriving open societies in which democracy and liberty flourished despite the menacing Iron Curtain to the east. The Marshall plan prevented millions of Europeans from starving to death as well as rebuilt destroyed homes and public services like water and power supplies. Notwithstanding the great example set by the "idealistic" Marshall Plan, conservatives continued to adhere

---

[61] The U.S.S.R., a non-participant in the Marshall Plan, took over Eastern Europe and the Marshall Plan could not prevent the decay of those societies, which was starkly on display in the late 1980s and early 1990s when the Iron Curtain came down.

to the doctrine of "Realpolitik" even in the face of it resulting in the death of tens of thousands of people in the developing and third world during the second half of the twentieth century as wars of independence raged all around the globe.

Furthermore, the Marshall Plan should have served as an example for America and the European powers to do something similar in Africa, Asia, South America, and the rest of North America (i.e. Central America and the Caribbean) considering the United States' and Europe's complicity in those regions' problems ranging from economic exploitation that wiped out subsistence economies as the people began to produce goods primarily for European and American markets to destructive colonial policies that led to the collapse of traditional/local/tribal governments that provided political stability leading to all out warfare in the aftermath of the Europeans withdrawing.

Piggybacking on the Marshall Plan, the United States could have encouraged the European colonial powers, in the wake of World War II, to begin a process of acknowledging the right of self-determination of their African, Asian, and Western Hemispheric colonies by establishing transitional executive and legislative councils to begin the process of democratization. Instead, this issue was ignored and within less than a decade after World War II colonial peoples throughout the world began to rebel against their imperial masters.[62] For example, Algerian and Vietnamese freedom fighters fought the French in an attempt to expel them from their lands and Egyptian nationalist drove the occupying British out of their country.

Instead of trying to bring an end to colonialism and establishing open democracies in the newly liberated nations of Africa and Asia using its great influence, the United States found itself allied with murderous dictators left in the wake of defeated imperial armies. Dictators like the late President Mobutu Sese Seko of former Zaire, now Democratic Republic of Congo, who appealed to the United States because he opposed the efforts of Communists to gain a foothold in his country but Sese Seko also killed millions with violence and starvation as he plundered the Congo's natural resources for his own personal gain. This is but

---

[62] Many historians attribute this mass rebellion in Africa and Asia to the success of the Japanese on the battlefield against the United Kingdom and the United States. The Japanese military machine purposefully put captured Allied troops on display for local peoples throughout Asia in an effort to disprove their assertions of European racial superiority.

one of the examples of the United States government choosing the wrong side under the doctrine of "Realpolitik."

We will examine a few other examples of America's entanglement with despotic regimes to establish the breadth and depth of the United States' involvement in the subjugation and murder of millions across the globe as a result of that conservative philosophy of turning a blind eye to America's so-called allies who commit atrocities against local populations and rule with iron fists simply because of their asserted willingness to oppose Communism. The first example we will survey is Iran, which has had a tumultuous relationship with the United States for much of the twentieth century.

Iran is a nation-state whose people are largely ethnic Persians, though there are numerous other smaller ethnic groups, who predominately practice Shia Islam. The country is located in the heart of Southwest Asia on the eastern edge of the region known as the Middle East. It is considered by many as the cradle of Western civilization as the early Europeans originated here before migrating to modern Europe. The United States and the United Kingdom[63] significantly interfered in the internal affairs of Iran during the height of the Cold War because of its proximity to the Soviet Union and its large oil and natural gas reserves. However, American and British involvement began much earlier.

While attempting to eject German Fuhrer Adolf Hitler's forces from Eastern Europe, the Allies asked Reza Shah Pahlavi, the King of Iran, to use Iranian territory as a staging ground for Allied troops and equipment. After being refused access to Iranian territory, Allied forces invaded Iran and forced Reza Shah Pahlavi to abdicate his throne in favor of his pro-Western son, Mohammad Reza Pahlavi. The new Shah (king) permitted the Allies to keep troops on Iranian soil and transport weapons to the Soviet Union to fight Nazi Germany on the eastern front. Mohammad Reza's actions made him appear to be a puppet of the Western powers to many Iranian citizens and parliamentarians who believed that this was only the beginning of outsiders trying to control the internal affairs of Iran, a country of fiercely independent people since the ancient times that were once a superpower of the ancient world.

In response to this interference in Iranian domestic affairs, a nationalist movement that adopted some Communist ideals for reforming the Iranian government and economy to ensure that Iranian resources benefited Iranians began to take root. Just as the

---

[63] British involvement extended back even further; perhaps 150 or more years.

barons of England forcing King John to sign the Magna Carta changed that nation from an absolute monarchy to a constitutional monarchy, the nationalists in Iran also attempted reign in the power of their king. In the mid-1940s, these Iranian nationalists began to challenge the Shah's use of his authority arbitrarily because it often benefited British interests over the national interests. In particular, the British controlled Iran's petroleum industry through the Anglo-Iranian Oil Company through agreements made with Mohammad Reza.[64]

Dr. Mohammed Mossadegh,[65] who demanded an end to British control of the petroleum industry and influence over the Iran's internal affairs, led the nationalist movement by using his persuasiveness and charisma to unite the various nationalist factions. Mossadegh successfully unified academics, intellectuals, religious clerics, and tradesmen in their efforts to reign in the shah and turf out the British, which led to his coalition receiving a parliamentary majority early in the 1950s. With the majority in the Majlis (parliament), the first challenge for the nationalist coalition was getting Mohammed Reza to appoint Mossadegh prime minister. By a lopsided majority, the Majlis presented Mossadegh to the shah as its choice for prime minister; essentially ensuring Mossadegh's appointment.

Once Mohammed Reza conceded and appointed Mossadegh prime minister, Mossadegh made several reforms to the Iranian economy including, with a vote of the Majlis, the nationalization of the Iranian petroleum industry in 1951. These reforms made western governments, in particular the United States and the United Kingdom, see Mossadegh as a Communist threat because they believed he would eventually align with the Soviet Union. In response, the British established a blockade of Iranian ports to prevent the export of any petroleum, which was disastrous to the Iranian economy.

In their battle to stem the spread of international Communism, Western powers began to plan for the removal of Mossadegh. With the blessing of Prime Minister Winston Churchill and President Dwight D. Eisenhower, American and British intelligence agencies engaged in joint operations to oust Mossadegh as prime minister. At the behest of the CIA and MI6

---

[64] Today this company is known as British Petroleum.
[65] Mossadegh, born in 1882, became involved in politics early in life by joining the growing number of Iranians who wanted to reign in the Shah's arbitrary use of power by adopting a constitution to limit that power.

operatives, the shah fled into exile to Italy in 1953. The intelligence agencies provided weapons to pro-monarchists and antagonized enemies of Mossadegh, in particular religious clerics.[66] This antagonism consisted of spreading rumors about how Mossadegh would not tolerate any dissent from the clerics and that they would be punished for engaging in any defiance. This created the intended rift between the nationalists and clerics who had allied in their opposition to the shah.

With the economy falling apart because of the petroleum blockade, his allies turning against him, and the prime minister's residence under military assault, Mossadegh stepped down as prime minister and the shah returned to power. Mossadegh served 3 years in prison for treason and spent the rest of his life in house arrest under the shah's rule. The shah consolidated power throughout the late 1950s and 1960s after he returned from self-imposed exile in Italy putting an end to Iran's fledgling constitutional-democratization movement. The returned oil revenues paid for military equipment to strengthen the secret police (SAVAK) and army, which led to a crackdown on free press and free speech with dissidents being imprisoned or forced into exile to avoid imprisonment and the weakening of the Majlis. With the liberal constitutional-democratization movement dead, a huge vacuum opened in Iran's opposition; where one opponent of the shah was silenced (Mossadegh) another one rose up to replace it (right-wing religious clerics).

As the Shah became increasingly repressive, the opposition, led by Islamic right-wingers, responded with massive demonstrations throughout the 1960s and 1970s. These demonstrations, just as those in the late 1940s and early 1950s, saw a united opposition to the Shah's arbitrary authority from all sectors of society. The demonstrations included university students, industrial workers, intellectuals and academics, and religious clerics. The difference this time was that right-wing Islamic fundamentalists led the movement as opposed to the liberalizing pro-democracy nationalists like Mossadegh of the 1940s and 1950s. It is interesting to note that during the demonstrations of the 1960s and 1970s a common rallying cry was what had happened to Mossadegh at the hands of the Shah and foreign powers.

By the late 1970s, the demonstrations had grown so large

---

[66] The clerics helped eliminate the biggest threat to them in Mossadegh and today they dominate that entire society.

that the Shah could no longer control the country. In January 1979, Mohammad Shah left Iran for exile in Mexico. His government fell in February. After discovering that he was ill, the Shah entered the United States, with the permission of President James Earl Carter, for medical treatment in October. In November 1979, Iranian revolutionaries stormed the American embassy in Tehran in protest of the United States allowing the Shah to receive medical treatment and not turning him over to Iranian authorities. They held the embassy's occupants hostage saying that they would only be released when the United States returned the Shah to Iran to stand trial. Of course, the United States refused to return him.

For the most part, the revolutionaries were a diverse body of Iranians. However, with the Muslim clerics filling the leadership vacuum, they were poised to assume control of the revolutionary government that, at the time, had immense popular support. The clerics united under the charismatic Ayatollah Ruhollah Khomeini, who had returned from exile abroad. Khomeini declared Iran an Islamic republic and appointed himself the supreme leader (faqih). Khomeini created a transitional government in the form of the Revolutionary Council. This new government put hundreds of officials from the previous government to death by firing squad, shuttered all free newspapers and magazines, banned political parties and unions, closed universities, and imposed Sharia law. This regime turned out to be just as, if not more, repressive than the previous one. It is interesting that the American and British government never saw the conservative (right-wing) Muslim clerics as a threat because they were too focused on the left-leaning nationalist leader Dr. Mohammad Mossadegh. Additionally, American and British interference in the political development of Iran bears much, if not all, of the responsibility for the group of repressive theocrats that currently govern that country.

Many Americans wrongfully blame President Carter for the embassy being stormed when the real culprit was the conservative American foreign policy decisions of prior administrations that strayed from the basic principles of international law and the core American principles upon which our society stands as well as having too narrow a focus on Communism. For example, one key and longstanding precept of international law is that one nation should not get involved in the internal affairs of another nation with a few limited exceptions such as preventing genocide. Since genocide was not an issue in pre-revolutionary Iran under Mossadegh's leadership, the United States and United Kingdom had no cause for interfering in Iran's internal affairs; not even the stalking specter of Communism justified such heavy-handedness, which ultimately led to the destruction of the fledgling democracy that was developing in Iran.[67]

American leaders supported Mohammad Reza Shah's hold on power in Iran assuring the death of the development of a plural liberal democratic republic. The Shah did not permit dissent, rely on the consent of the governed (the people), or cooperate with the people's representatives in the Majlis. Instead, the Shah ruled with an iron fist. America and Britain sided with this despot in his grasp for absolute power at the expense of the Iranian people. It is these actions that led to the intransigence of the Iranian people, even those who are opposed to the despotic clerics in charge. Instead of standing for what our Founding Fathers believed, our leadership stood for what was the most expedient at the time. What we now know is that America's reputation with the people of the Middle East has been severely damaged by these actions.

A cornerstone of American foreign policy should always be that the United States supports the people of other nations freely choosing their own governments regardless of what our government thinks about their (the people's) choice. We cannot talk about promoting multiparty democracy while we are taking actions that are directly opposed to that concept. Of course, with the current state of affairs in many Middle Eastern nations, right-wing extremists are sure to win elections if they were held today; this is largely the result of decades of repression, which oftentimes leads to repressed people making extremist choices in elections. However, transitioning to multiparty democracies with open public debate and free press outlets is not impossible as exemplified by the Republic of Turkey.

Kemal Ataturk deliberately set out on a path to neutralize the power of conservative, religious clerics by liberalizing Turkish society. Ataturk did this by extending to women the right to vote, get educations, work outside the home, not have to wear religious dress, and run as candidates for elective office. While Turkey is no perfect example (no country is, not even the United States), it is an example because Turkish women are afforded the greatest freedom in the Middle East or any majority Muslim country, which was exemplified with Tansu Ciller becoming prime minister in 1993.

---

[67] Considering the interests that British oil companies had in Iran's oilfields under the Shah it is not impracticable to believe that oil was the real reason for Western interference in that country's affairs.

Turkish success in becoming an open, democratic society is largely due to the efforts of Ataturk and other domestic reformers who marshaled the forces necessary to subdue narrow-minded religious extremists. External interference rarely assists reformers in turning back extremists bent on creating an ideological vacuum of despotism and authoritarianism.

The current Bush regime has stated that it will support Iranian reformers in their battle to promote civil liberties in the right-wing hardline Islamic Republic of Iran.[68] The plan includes spending tens of millions to promote democracy in Iran. However, the reform activists in Iran have said that the Bush Administration's plan have only increased the scrutiny that activists face in Iran with some being arrested and interrogated for days and imprisonment for promoting human and civil rights. Additionally, the current right-wing Iranian regime is empowered to argue that the "Great Satan" is attempting to subdue Iran as it once did in the 1940s turning the Iranian people and their resources into American-owned commodities.

Bush's plan proves the continued arrogance and ignorance of the conservative movement in America. Their leadership does not examine the long-term effects of their policies and programs. Even though their interference will probably strengthen the control of the theocratic regime, American conservatives persist in interfering in the internal affairs of Iran resulting the torture, imprisonment, and death of hundreds, if not thousands, of Iranian reformers. With the assistance of the conservative despots currently in charge in Washington, D.C., the success of the Iranian clerics in maintaining their control on the country is almost assured. Conservative interference in the domestic affairs of other nations did not end with Iran.

In South America, the United States' conservative leaders engaged in anti-democratic activities in their fight against Communism in several different countries. From Guatemala to Panama, El Salvador to Costa Rica, the United States engaged in activity that oftentimes saw the superpower siding with dictators or potential dictators as the local populations elected nationalist leaders who wanted to expel American corporations from their nations and adopt socialists programs for their economies. One particular target was Chile. Chile is a country of about 16 million people that is located on the Western coast of the South American

---

[68] Vick, Karl and David Finkel, "Activists in Iran say U.S. strategy hurts their work," *The Seattle Times (Washington Post)*, March 14, 2006.

continent and is known for its fantastic peaks and gauchos. Chile is also known because of the thousands of *Disappeared*. These were individuals, some Chilean and some not, who were leftist activists, politicians, and union members that were forcibly removed from society by the Chilean military junta led by Augusto Pinochet because their political beliefs; many of them were never heard from again.

In 1970, Dr. Salvador Allende Gossens was elected Chilean president. Allende campaigned on the basis that his government would create a socialist state that would lift everyone out of poverty using the nation's natural resources. Allende's election made him the first socialist elected president of a country in the Western Hemisphere. Under his leadership, the government embarked on an ambitious mission to institute the promised program by nationalizing banks and mines as well as adopting sweeping land reforms. These reforms, intended to assist the 'have-nots,' drew sharp opposition from the 'haves' of society. Allende's election and policies did not go unnoticed by the United States' conservative regime.

The Nixon Administration began plotting against Allende as soon as the Chilean people elected him president by attempting to stop the Chilean Congress from confirming his election. "Richard Nixon and Henry Kissinger were determined to remove Allende from power once the Chilean congress had done the unimaginable by voting to confirm the Socialist president-elect. Indeed, successive administrations dating back to 1958 had been desperate to prevent his election"[69] as U.S. funding was given to Allende's political rivals for use in their campaigns against him.

President Richard M. Nixon, on September 15, 1970, authorized the use of nearly $10,000,000 to prevent Allende from ever taking power after several days of meetings with his national security staff[70] concluded that Allende was a threat because of his leftist views and a U.S. sponsored Chilean military coup d'etat was the only way to stop him. First, the United States cutoff all aid to the Chilean government. However, Allende received support from the Soviet Union and Cuba. The CIA and the United States Ambassador to Chile then began to encourage and support right-wing forces within the Chilean armed forces to take swift and

---

[69] Mark Escalasco, *Chile Under Pinochet: Recovering the Truth*, (Philadelphia: University of Pennsylvania Press, 2000), 156.
[70] National Security Advisor Henry Kissinger, Director of Central Intelligence Richard Helms, and Attorney General John Mitchell all attended this meeting.

certain action against Allende. Not all Chilean officers were onboard with ousting the democratically-elected Allende. One in particular, General Rene Schneider, was assessed by the U.S. ambassador as an impediment to the coup's success and that he needed to be neutralized. Subsequently, General Schneider was kidnapped, tortured, and murdered to clear the way for the successful removal of President Allende. On September 11, 1973, the army took control of the country by attacking the presidential palace and preventing Allende's escape. The initial reports were that Allende committed suicide rather than surrender to his enemies but many believe that Allende was assassinated[71] by his opponents.

A military junta took control of Chile and immediately dissolved Congress, shuttered the free press, banned political parties, and shutdown the labor and land reform organizations started by Allende's popular coalition. The junta set about eliminating its opponents so that there would be no opposition. This included the peasant activists and labor union leaders. For example, General Sergio Arellano Stark, on the orders of General Augusto Pinochet, traveled the Chilean countryside where he systematically hunted down leftists and murdered them.[72] Thousands of people were either tortured or murdered or both by this new American sponsored regime. Family members never knew what happened to their loved ones.[73]

General Augusto Pinochet Ugarte took over the reins of leadership of this junta and became president. Under Pinochet, the Chilean economy was structured to operate on a pure capitalist model with the assistance of a group of right-wing American economists known as the Chicago Boys. Pinochet eliminated most social programs and tariffs on imports. Wages collapsed, businesses shut their doors, and starvation became a real daily threat for the average Chilean. During all of this, the United States gave massive amounts of aid to Pinochet's regime.

On the political front, in 1980, Pinochet's idea of constitutional reform was to increase the powers of the president, formalize the military's role in governmental affairs, prohibit a future government from adopting socialist programs, and made Pinochet the permanent head of the army. However, this new

---

[71] The Chilean military coup leaders said that Allende committed suicide.
[72] E.g. Escalasco, *Chile Under Pinochet*, 39-44.
[73] The families of the missing and murdered began to refer to them as "The Disappeared" because it was as if they had vanished from the face of the earth.

constitution did include a provision for a plebiscite in 1988 on whether Pinochet should continue on as president. Between 1980 and 1988, Pinochet continued to crackdown on his opponents in an effort to discourage dissent. In 1988, Pinochet lost the plebiscite, which led to the election of a new president and Congress in 1989. 1989 also saw the Chilean people vote for a return of civil liberties to their constitution. Though no longer Chile's president, Pinochet had solidified his hold on power continuing on as head of the army until 1998 when he became a senator for life.

During the military junta's reign of death to consolidate its control, the Nixon Administration abandoned any appearance of attempting to adhere to America's core principles. Nixon's government supported the military overthrow of the democratically-elected civilian government on the basis that its leaders had a different political philosophy than our own. Our own system of government subordinates the military to the control of the civilian government. That is to say the president hires and fires the military commanders and Congress decides how much, if any, funding the military receives as exemplified by President Truman's firing of General McArthur for insubordination yet, in Chile Nixon supported a military takeover of a government and society despite the Chilean people freely choosing its own leader.

These types of decisions place America at a disadvantage because our leaders are saying that they support plural, liberal, representative democratic government but their actions prove otherwise. The rest of the world distrusts our nation and, in some instances, becomes our enemies as a result of decisions like these; decisions that result in the death of thousands of innocent persons while presidents like Ronald Reagan declare their fondness for dictators like Pinochet.[74] During Pinochet's regime, "conservatives in Congress, led by the arch-conservative Senator Jesse Helms of North Carolina, managed to lift the ban on military assistance" to Chile.[75] As late as the 1980s, America's conservative leadership continued to support the overthrow of popular and democratically-elected officials in other countries such as Nicaragua.

The conservative Reagan Administration meddled in the internal affairs of Nicaragua because a popularly-supported leftist guerilla movement overthrew the long-reigning (though stabilizing), pro-American dictatorial dynasty of the Somozas.[76] Nicaragua is a

---

[74] See Escalasco, *Chile Under Pinochet*, 162.
[75] Id. at 163.

small country located on the southern portion of the North American continent in a region known as Central America. The Sandinista National Liberation Front,[77] a guerilla group led by Daniel Ortega, militarily defeated the decades-long dictatorship of the Somoza family in 1979. The Sandinistas forced the Somozas into exile abroad. The Sandinista government nationalized huge portions of the economy and adopted social programs to assist the poor who were suffering as a result of the civil war and the economic policies of the Somoza regime. The social programs included better healthcare and newly built schools. In 1981, the Reagan Administration responded by cutting off aid to the Nicaraguan government and began to encourage and aid former Somoza government officials, a.k.a. the Contras, to rebel against the Sandinistas. These Contras began raids into Nicaragua from their hideouts in Honduras. The United States provided funding to the Contras while the Soviet Union, Cuba, and some Western European nations provided funding to the Nicaraguan government.

Reagan stepped up his attacks on the Sandinistas in the wake of Daniel Ortega winning a free and fair presidential election, according to international observers, in 1984 by declaring that the Sandinistas had established a Communist regime and needed to be stopped. Thus, began the United States government's support for

---

[76] The United States role in Nicaragua actually dates back to 1901 when the United States attempted to build a canal through Nicaragua. Nicaraguan President Jose Santos Zelaya limited American control over any future canal through his country, which forced the United States to withdraw the plan and head to Panama. Since then, the United States has actively involved itself in the affairs of that country. For example,

- In 1909, during a civil insurrection against Zelaya, the United States supported the rebels
- In 1912, U.S. Marines were sued to repel a rebellion led by Nicaraguans opposed to U.S. involvement in the nations internal affairs. These Marines remained in the country for over two decades after the initial invasion
- From 1927 to 1933, General Augusto Cesar Sandino and his rebel army launched guerilla attacks on the Marines in an attempt to force the Marines to leave Nicaragua.

[77] The rebel movement was named for General Augusto Cesar Sandino who was murdered in 1934 by National Guard General Anastasio Somoza Garcia. The National Guard had been trained by the United States Marines. Somoza took control of the country in 1936 declaring himself president and his family ruled Nicaragua until 1979.

terrorists and murders. The Reagan Administration assisted the Contras in placing anti-ship mines in Nicaraguan ports and waterways in addition to placing an embargo on all economic activity with Nicaragua nearly destroying the nation's economy and hurting the people of that nation immensely.[78]

The Administration continued all of its support despite the Congress passing a law in October 1984 prohibiting all aid to the Contras. The Administration decided to sell weapons to the Iranian government in its war with Iraq with the funds going to support the Contras in Nicaragua. Not only did this illegal activity lead to many indictments of Reagan government officials, but the war will have a long lasting effect on the Nicaraguan people in that many innocent people were maimed or killed as the Contras attempted to overthrow the democratically-elected Sandinista government because of Reagan's poor decision making.

Additionally, not since President Andrew Johnson's ignoring the Congress, has a president ignored an explicit statutory prohibition imposed by the Congress; thus, setting the stage for George W. Bush's even more obscene violations of international law and U.S. law. The war ended in June 1990 with a cease fire agreement between the Nicaraguan government and the Contras but the effects of that war will be long lasting. Under the auspices of the Reagan Administration, this pattern repeated itself all across Central America with the Reagan Administration supporting right-wing militant terrorist organizations that had been rejected at the polls by the local populations but did not accept the results and chose to change the result by going to war.

While those are three of the most egregious examples of conservative foreign policy gone awry, there are many other instances in which our conservative-dominated foreign policy linked America to homicidal dictators in the interest of fighting Communism or some other boogeyman that merely serves as a stalking horse to promote the right-wing agenda of expanding corporate power to other shores and the strengthening the military-industrial complex around the globe at the expense of others.

In the 1980s, Reagan and Iraqi President Saddam Hussein were close allies. In fact, Reagan sent his special envoy Donald Rumsfeld to meet with Hussein, which can be seen in old archive video footage as Hussein greets Rumsfeld in Baghdad with a smile

---

[78] In 1986, the International Court of Justice ruled that the United States violated international law in siding with the Contras by providing military aid and for assisting with the mining.

on December 20, 1983. Several other top Reagan Administration officials would pay visits to Hussein's Iraq to show support for him during the war with Iran even while Hussein was massacring the Kurds and we were secretly and illegally selling weapons to the Iranians.

Hussein, a secular Middle Eastern despot, was embroiled in a bitter war with the Islamic Republic of Iran that lasted eight years. During this war, Hussein used poison gases on Iranian military forces but the Reagan Administration did not take any action to address Hussein's violation of international law. This historical roadmap shows the missteps, contradictions, and malfeasance inherent in operating under a conservative foreign policy based on Realpolitik rather than promoting human rights, civil rights, and equal rights ideals that arise from our four fundamental principles. Nevertheless, it still appears that our conservative leaders have not learned their lesson.

The current conservative Bush Administration has hijacked America's foreign policy. President George W. Bush is going even further than past conservative administrations in destroying America's reputation as a beacon for pluralism, liberalism, democracy, and republicanism throughout the world. Instead, Bush has chosen to promote nationalism at home to advance his imperialistic and militaristic foreign policy abroad. The administration has done this through a myriad of unlawful actions such as (1) launching a preemptive war on Iraq based on intelligence that was made up citing Saddam Hussein's stockpile of chemical and biological agents even though weapons inspectors could not locate any,[79] (2) disregarding conservative White House Counterterrorism expert Richard Clarke's warning about the dangers of Al Qaeda before the September 11, 2001 attacks while searching for a reason for war with Iraq, (3) ignoring well-settled international law on prisoners of war in favor of creating a new enemy combatant status for Taliban soldiers which endangers American military personnel because future enemies may decide that they are not entitled to POW protections either, and (4) threatening to launch military attacks on the only independent media outlet in the Middle East, Al Jazeera, because it refuses to promote American propaganda like Fox News. Because of

---

[79] There has also been talk of promoting the spread of democracy and saving Iraqis from Hussein. If that were truly the case, American troops would be on the ground in Sudan preventing the Islamic government of the north from slaughtering the largely Christian black Africans of the south.

President Bush's actions, instead of the United States being viewed as a beacon of light in the rest of the world, our country is seen as a serious threat to world stability, both political and economic.

With our government continuing to violate international law and disregarding the rights of other world citizens to live their lives free from American interference, many Americans still wonder why so many people around the world dislike or hate the United States. Conservative President George W. Bush's response in the wake of the September 11 Al Qaeda attacks was "they hate our freedoms."[80] The "liberal media" in the form of television and talk radio promoted this explanation in the aftermath of the attacks adding to the ignorance and confusion that many Americans already have about the rest of the world because we already know so little about the other people who share this planet with us as shown in poll after poll proving the failure of the American educational system.

Notwithstanding the overly simplistic and ignorant nature of President Bush's explanation, the fact that the "liberal media" advanced this lunacy proves that conservatives have control of the "liberal media" through its corporate executives who are overwhelmingly conservatives. Notwithstanding them knowingly keeping the American public in the dark, conservatives are aware that it is our foreign policy decisions that have made the United States a pariah around the world. So long as our foreign policy decisions are inconsistent with the principles upon which our republic was founded, America will continue to garner the hatred and disdain of the other people with whom we share this planet.

Because we have allowed conservatives to hijack our foreign policy, we also face the continued threat of more terrorist attacks over the next several years or decades even. In particular, Middle Eastern militants pose a significant threat to the United States as they are able to recruit new, radical and fearless members as a result of conservative foreign policy missteps. Not only have these foreign policy missteps led to young Arabs enlisting into terrorist organizations but it has also led to American John Walker Lindh and Australian David Hicks also joining militant movements against the United States. More of this can be expected in the future unless the United States throws off the shackles of conservatism and focuses on the real issues that cause this militancy.

---

[80] President George W. Bush, Address to a Joint Session of Congress and the American People, September 20, 2001.

The central point of focus is the conflict between the Palestinians and Israel. While the U.S. has rightfully recognized the existence of the state of Israel and demanded that Palestinians do the same, conservative presidential administrations have failed to strenuously demand that Israel withdraw from the occupied territories and the West Bank, stop building settlements on Palestinian lands, as well as, most controversially, recognize the right of return for all Palestinians who fled their homes in Israel to refugee camps during the wars between the fledgling Israel and numerous Arab states. While I understand the fear of the Israeli government that their small population of Israeli Jews will be overrun by the larger population of Islamic Palestinian Arabs and will open the door to terrorists to carry out more successful attacks against the state of Israel, these are not valid justifications for preventing millions of people from returning to their homes based on ethnic stereotyping similar to that used by American white supremacist or Germany's Nazi party. It would be tantamount to the United States saying that because white supremacist organizations like the Ku Klux Klan or the Aryan Nations are all white, all white Americans should be prevented from going to some parts of the United States for fear they may carryout hate crimes such as lynchings against African Americans.

While the right of return may be wholly unworkable logistically, there may be some room for the United States, the United Kingdom, France, and other western powers to provide economic development assistance to the Palestinians in the form of power plants, water treatment/reclamation facilities, and medical centers (a Mid-East Marshall Plan) in exchange for the Palestinian Authority capitulating on the right of return as well as the partitioning of Jerusalem. The point is that the western powers who are responsible for creating this quandary in the Middle East should take the lead in resolving it, which has the effect of taking the wind out of the sails of the militants. If the Palestinian Authority refuses to cooperate on something as sensible as this, then the western powers should put the proposed plan to a referendum before the Palestinian people under the auspices of the United Nations. There has to be a resolution that can be reached because the current plan of the state of Israel is not working.

The current plan of military suppression and isolation has failed miserably at stopping Palestinian militants from carrying out bombings. Suicide bombings have continued to wreak havoc on the Israeli civilian population. The only real way to bring an end to America being a pariah in the Middle East is for the United States to take an evenhanded approach to dealing with both Israel and the Palestinians regardless of which political organization represents them (i.e. Hamas). This, coupled with a strong military and/or law enforcement response to acts of terrorism, will go a long way toward deflating the willingness of young Arabs to join terrorist organizations bent on taking American lives and destroying American property as well as make Israelis safer in the long run. There is no way to stop all terrorist attacks or prevent all persons from joining hate groups as demonstrated here in the United States with several thousand white Americans joining white supremacist organizations or militia groups because of some perceived threat from others who look different and speak different languages. The overarching point is that only through reforming our foreign policy can we isolate terrorist groups making their recruitment efforts nearly impossible thus jeopardizing their very existence. A prosperous people who have employment, own homes, and enjoy life with their families do not generally join terrorist organizations but an impoverished people trapped in serfdom have nothing to lose. The United States needs to take the lead for any of these to happen.

One significant step would be for the president of the United States to apologize to those people who have suffered from our government's past foreign policy decisions that adversely affected local populations. For example, an apology should be directed to the oppressed people of Iran for our support of the Shah's brutal regime, which led directly to the current regime of religious fanatics that refuse to allow the people to govern themselves. This would only be the first step to reforming American foreign policy. Additional action plans can be developed that are consistent with our foreign policy goal of promoting plural liberal democratic republics throughout the world. Perhaps it is time for a democratizing Marshall Plan for Africa and Asia with the goal of bringing electricity, clean water, medical care, and education to people in places like the Democratic Republic of Congo and Cambodia. It is time America walked the walk of what we stand for as opposed to being sucked into the game of Realpolitik where we only create future enemies that are oftentimes not foreseeable (i.e. Mujahedeen elements became the Taliban). This is a game that, in the end, no one will win.

CHAPTER 5: CONSERVATISM & WHITE SUPREMACY: TWO PEAS IN A POD

Conservatives have a long history of engaging in racism a.k.a. white supremacy in particular. Understanding that conservatism is built on the concept of protecting the status quo or society's traditions, it is abundantly clear that conservatives would even protect those traditions that are detrimental to the liberty of others like people of color (i.e. nonwhites). Underlying this desire to protect worthless and invidiously racial traditions, is a latent, and sometimes patent, belief that white Americans are superior (based on culture, history, and biology) to others, which is known as white supremacy. Because of this inherent inequality between the races (at least that is what white supremacists would argue), nonwhites were not permitted to engage in many of the same activities that white Americans took for granted.

In the aftermath of the Civil War and Reconstruction, African Americans suffered nearly 100 years of Jim Crow segregation and Ku Klux Klan terrorism.[81] This was unlike any discrimination faced by white immigrants coming to America because they were often allowed to join society because of their white skin whereas African Americans had their dark skin color as a major impediment to their integration in American society as well as Jim Crow's spotlight on that dark skin color. Thus, for my fellow Americans of European ancestry there is no comparator of

---

[81] Reconstruction ended in 1876, which saw Jim Crow legislation passed all across the south and it did not end until the late 1960s and early 1970s in much of this country.

white immigrants initial struggles in America to the evil perpetuated by Jim Crow and white America against African Americans.

With that being said, Jim Crow segregation was both de facto and de jure. It was de facto in the sense that society had certain unwritten cultural customs and norms that limited the activities of African Americans. African Americans routinely had to give way on sidewalks to allow whites to pass and traditionally could not look whites in the eye for fear of being lynched for being uppity. Jim Crow was de jure in that many state governments adopted laws that prohibited African Americans from engaging in activities that the average white American did on a day-to-day basis. For example, Jim Crow prohibited interracial marriages, Blacks from serving on juries, using certain public accommodations (i.e. restrooms, restaurants, movie theaters, and hotels), living in certain neighborhoods, working in certain professions, and testifying against white men on trial just to name a few. Entire generations of African Americans went from living and dying as slaves to living and dying as noncitizens during this 100-year period of Jim Crow despite the adoption of the Fourteenth Amendment, which was intended to extend the benefits of citizenship to African Americans.

In fact, my generation of African Americans is the first to be truly free in America to pursue and live our dreams free from the social and legal constrictions faced by my mother and grandmother. Prior generations of African Americans had to deal with trying to survive and avoid falling victim to the raping, maiming, and murdering committed by angry lynch mobs, white riots (i.e. Rosewood, Florida), or KKK night riders visiting African Americans who were perceived to be trying to disturb the established tradition of the south. The Jim Crow period in American history represents pure racism. The overarching point here, however, is not what Jim Crow was but that southern conservatives sought to protect this tradition at the expense of African Americans simply because they believed that it was preordained by their twisted sense of what God intended.

Despite this damning history and the insidious nature of Jim Crow staring conservatives in the face, many contemporary conservative leaders continue to deny the complicity of their ilk in trying to maintain the ill-conceived racial segregation that the white southern aristocracy depended on to continue their traditional domination of African Americans and poor southern whites. Additionally, they also do not recognize the necessity of the Civil Rights movement in changing America. For example, former conservative Senator Jesse Helms (R-NC) recently assailed the Civil Rights movement for moving too fast in demanding equality. Helms believed that the Civil Rights movement caused too much upheaval and disturbed the order of society causing instant and monumental changes to American society before whites were ready to accept it. The problem with Helms' position is that it fails to recognize that African Americans had tried to implement a plan for integration over a period of several decades going back to the end of Reconstruction and that several hundred thousand Americans died (more than in any other war) to protect this nation in face of an evil empire known as the Confederate States of America attempting to destroy the United States for their own selfish, greedy, and immoral desires.

Another important oversight by conservatives like Helms is that prolonged racial divisiveness leads to hatred of the oppressor, acceptance of the division as natural, dehumanization of the oppressed, and violent backlashes directed at the oppressor. Many of these same characteristics can be seen in other societies that adopted similar programs of racial/ethnic/religious segregation that included some of the previously mentioned prohibitions and restrictions that I mentioned earlier as being typical of American Jim Crow segregation. As shown in Apartheid South Africa and Nazi Germany, oppression stunts the economic, social, and political development of the oppressed and creates fear in the oppressors that one day the dehumanized oppressed will strike back with violence intended to turn the tables so the oppressors continue to increase the amount of force they are willing to use to maintain control. Notwithstanding the lessons modern American conservatives could take away from our own Civil War and Civil Rights movement as well as Apartheid South Africa and Nazi Germany, American conservatives can also learn lessons from early American history about the division caused by continuing to advance a racist ideology.

Conservatives in America have worked from the very beginning to protect and advance a racist status quo. At the Philadelphia Constitutional Convention in 1787, southern conservatives opposed any effort to end slavery as the delegates debated creating a society that supposedly protected the individual's right to life, liberty, and the pursuit of happiness. Instead, conservatives sought and received three constitutional provisions that protected the institution of slavery. One clause required the return of runaway slaves from Free states to Slave states and their masters precluding any claim of freedom as a result of reaching free soil.[82] Another clause required slaves be counted as three-fifths of a person for the purpose of the census and taxation, which provided southerners with the benefit of additional representation in the House of Representatives while simultaneously limiting the amount of federal taxes paid by southern states.[83] Still another clause prohibited Congress from ending the United States participation in the Atlantic slave trade until at least 1808. These protections for the South's Peculiar Institution still did not satisfy southern slavers as they sought further benefits and concessions from the nation for their abhorrent and immoral activity.

For much of the first half of the 1800s, Congress enacted legislation in an attempt to appease southern conservatives who worried that an expanding nation would eventually isolate the few southern Slave states resulting in their eventually being dominated by a congressional supermajority of Free states that would threaten their Peculiar Institution. From the Missouri Compromise of 1820, the Wilmot Proviso of 1846, the Compromise of 1850, the Kansas-Nebraska Act of 1854, the Congress attempted to address the issue in various ways as abolitionist forces faced off with pro-slavery conservatives from the south. Nevertheless, nothing ended the division between the two sides leading to the aforementioned Civil War as well as the adoption of the Thirteenth, Fourteenth, and Fifteenth Amendments. Despite all of this historical evidence showing conservatives involvement in nearly destroying this Great Republic, contemporary conservatives, including a cohesive majority of white Americans, continued to oppose the advancement of people of color during much of the twentieth century with the only real difference being their change in party affiliation as will be discussed shortly. The broader point is that for decades in the early and mid-twentieth century, conservatives opposed any legislation to end Jim Crow's stranglehold on the progress of African Americans. In fact, conservatives would dominate the politics of an entire region of the United States forestalling any effective change.

Conservative Democrats controlled what was known as the solid south; that is every state below the Mason-Dixon Line voted for the Democratic Party.[84] From the end of Reconstruction

---

[82] Article IV, Section 2, Clause 3 of the Constitution of the United States (1789). This clause was invalidated with the adoption of the Thirteenth Amendment in 1865.

[83] Article I, Section 2, Clause 3 of the Constitution of the United States (1789).

in 1876 to the 1960s, the Democratic Party dominated southern elections based, in part, on the perception that Abraham Lincoln and his radical Republican Party had destroyed and humiliated the south during the Civil War. This proved to be a potent recipe for conservatives to dominate the region. Indeed, in many southern states, the official election was the Democratic Party primary as any Republican candidates could only put up a token opposition at the general election.

While conservatives dominated the Democratic Party in the south, Democrats with progressive and forward looking points of view held office in other parts of the country under the party banner. This created a natural tension that was only exacerbated by the Civil Rights Movement's demand for racial equality in education, housing, employment, and other areas of society. The initial groundwork for the southern conservatives' break with the Democratic Party came in the late 1940's when President Harry S. Truman desegregated the United States Armed Forces on the basis that since African Americans were dying in the Korean police action just like white Americans they should die side-by-side. In response, conservative Democratic South Carolina Senator Strom Thurmond split with the Democratic Party to run for president under the Dixiecrat banner in protest of Truman's decision, which will be discussed further later. This was just the first of many perceived insults white southerners would suffer at the hands of so-called nigger lovers like Harry Truman.

Southern conservatives would experience further "insults" and "indignities" at the hands of so-called "outsiders" who were imposing their standards and social mores on the south. In 1954, the Supreme Court of the United States overturned 58 years of constitutional precedent in overruling *Plessy v. Ferguson*. In *Plessy*, the 1896 Court had ruled that having separate facilities on the basis of race was constitutionally permissible. However, the Warren Court saw this *Plessy* holding as extremely flawed in *Brown v. Board of Education of Topeka, Kansas*. The Court determined that separate school facilities on the basis of race inherently violated the Fourteenth Amendment's Equal Protection Clause, which guaranteed all persons within the United States the right to be treated the same as similarly situated persons. This decision was so controversial that southern states and the Ku Klux Klan

---

[84] The Mason-Dixon Line is a surveyor's line of the southern border of Pennsylvania (free state) and the northern borders of Maryland and Delaware (both slave states). This line served to divide the Slave states and the Free states.

resurrected the long-buried Confederate Battle Flag.[85] While Brown presented a huge problem for the unity of the national Democratic Party, the divide between conservative southern Democrats and their more moderate and progressive northern counterparts became unbridgeable with one solemn act of a former segregationist Texas politician turn national statesman.

Amid the increasing violence directed at Civil Rights activists, black and white, Democratic President Lyndon B. Johnson signed into law the Civil Rights Act of 1964. This legislation barred discrimination on the basis of race, color, national origin, religion, and sex in employment, public accommodations, and by participants in federal programs (i.e. those receiving federal funding) as well as criminalized some civil rights violations. The legislation also provided private legal remedies to those individuals who were the victims of such discrimination. President Johnson's action set off a firestorm of anger and rage across the south among whites because these changes truly marked the end of their tradition/social order; it signaled the death of Jim Crow segregation, dejure and de facto. The Civil Rights Act of 1964 became the straw that broke the camel's back for many southern whites. President Johnson recognized it, in a recorded Oval Office telephone call, almost immediately that his enactment of this legislation would result in the Democratic Party losing the south forever. He was right. White, conservative Democrats began to flee the party in droves, politician and others alike. Waiting to embrace these abandoned souls was the Republican Party.

In 1968, Presidential candidate Richard M. Nixon recognized that white southerners had had their world turned upside down with nearly a century of local tradition, custom, and practice as well as state laws relegated to the history books. Now, African Americans were able to eat, sleep, and shop in the same places as whites. Whites would be tried for committing crimes against African Americans unlike in the past. Nixon understood that white southerners were angered and confused. This presented the perfect opportunity for the Republican Party to gain ground on the Democratic Party in the south and he believed that the chaos of southern society was the right occasion to devise a plan to take

---

[85] Mississippi had been the only state to keep the Confederate Battle Flag as a part of its official state flag after the end of Reconstruction in 1876. Not even the Ku Klux Klan carried the flag until the 1954 Brown v. Board decision. Up until that point the KKK flew the American flag exclusively.

advantage of that anger and confusion.

So, Nixon's campaign talked about re-imposing "law and order" on a lawless society. To white conservative southerners, this meant stop the sit-ins, marches, and defiance of uppity African Americans. Nixon's campaign plan became known as the Southern Strategy. The overt message underlying the Southern Strategy was received loud and clear. Southerners who had long been faithful Democratic Party politicians and voters suddenly declared themselves Republicans taking with them their racial animosity toward African Americans. Since then, conservative Republicans in America have continued to employ Nixon's tactic, some even more crassly, and have turned a blind eye to overtly racist persons in their midst.

In a Nixonian fashion, conservatives continued into the late twentieth century to use racist messages, overt and covert, to appeal to white voters who had a penchant for hating racial minorities. In the 1980s, conservative Ronald Reagan made several speeches where he talked of Chicago welfare queens getting rich off of government aid instead of working hard like his nearly all white audiences. His audience understood that the code was for lazy African American women of Chicago who sat at home having children so that they could get more free government assistance at hard working white Americans' expense.

In 1988's presidential election, Vice President George H. W. Bush ran a political advertisement on television against his opponent Massachusetts Governor Michael Dukakis featuring a black and white photograph of an African American inmate who had murdered a person while out on furlough during Dukakis' gubernatorial administration suggesting that Dukakis would mean more Black-on-White crime; since the 1700s in the United States, white Americans have feared some supposed Slave/Black uprising in which whites are raped, maimed, and murdered by angered Slaves/Blacks out of vengeance for the atrocities and violence of slavery and Jim Crow respectively. The Bush campaign claimed that the intent of the advertisement was to portray Dukakis as weak on crime. However, the advertisement could have done that without using the photograph of convicted murderer Willie Horton, who, by the way, happened to be Africa American.

In 1990, Jesse Helms ran a campaign advertisement against his African American opponent former Charlotte Mayor Harvey Gantt where he capitalized on the racism of some of North Carolina's white population by depicting a white person losing a job to an unqualified African American based on a racial quota advanced by Gantt. Finally, as recently as 2000, conservative then Texas Governor George W. Bush's campaign started an underground attack against fellow Republican Arizona Senator John McCain alleging that he had a black child out of wedlock during the run-up to the South Carolina Republicans Party's selection of a Republican presidential nominee. These are examples of atrocious race-baiting by the former party of Lincoln and so called color-blindness attempting to excite white voters with racist tactics. Conservatives have learned that Nixon's tactics work effectively among white voters so there is no hesitancy to rely on racist tactics in elections but political advertisements are not the only place these unethical and immoral tactics have been employed.

In 1997, Senator Sam Brownback (R-KS) imitated a broken English, Asian accent when he said "no raise money, no get bonus" during a congressional investigation of Democratic fundraiser John Huang and his allegedly bringing Chinese government money into a U.S. election.[86] During the 2006 mid-term congressional election campaign, then Virginia Senator George Allen called a campaign volunteer for Democrat Jim Webb of ethnic Indian ancestry, who had been assigned to record the senator's speeches, a "macaca," which is a species of monkey from North Africa but also a pejorative term used in North Africa to refer to dark-skinned persons.[87] While the likes of former Secretary of State Madeleine Albright and others have appeared pleasantly surprised to learn that they had Jewish ancestry, Allen appeared visibly bothered by questions asked during a debate about his own Jewish ancestry in September 2006. A former University of Virginia football teammate of Allen's, Dr. Ken Shelton, told a story of Allen stuffing a severed deer head into an African American family's mailbox in the early 1970s. There are numerous other examples of conservatives engaging in Nixonian tactics intended to arouse racist feelings in white Americans in hopes that they would act on those unreasonable and un-American views by voting Republican. Nevertheless, presidential candidate George W. Bush claimed in 2000 that the Republican Party has a "Big Tent" that was "compassionate" and welcoming to all persons regardless of their race or ethnic background despite his conservative allies'

---

[86] Steven Thomma, "Senator Links Gift To Bank Of China -- Specter: $50,000 Came To Democrats," *Knight-Ridder Newspapers*, July 11, 1997.

[87] Craig, Tim and Michael D. Shear, "Senator says he's sorry for "macaca" comment," _Seattle Times (Washington Post)_, August 15, 2006.

failure to lay to rest the ghosts of their segregationists' pasts. In reality, a conservative southern politician's statement would come to exemplify the conservative movement's lack of compassion and "Small Tent" orientation of the party.

While attending the 100th birthday party of conservative Sen. Strom Thurmond (R-SC) in December 2002, Senator Trent Lott (R-MS) declared that if Thurmond had been elected president in 1948, paraphrasing, America would not have had all of these problems for all of these years. When questioned about the remarks, Lott clarified that he was talking about Thurmond's economic policies. The problem is that, as established earlier, Thurmond, then a conservative Democrat, ran for president as a Dixiecrat exclusively in protest of Democratic President Harry S. Truman's decision to desegregate the United States Armed Forces; Thurmond was entirely a single issue presidential candidate. Thurmond believed that President Truman was promoting race mixing that would ultimately lead to the destruction of the white race despite it later being discovered that Thurmond engaged in extramarital sexual relations with an African American woman that led to the birth of a child bi-racial child.

Initially, the "liberal" media ignored the U.S. Senate Majority Leader's comments. Only after some minor complaints did the larger "liberal" media pick of the story; even conservative Black-sellout Armstrong Williams spoke out about the remarks. In the aftermath, some called on Lott to resign as the Senate Majority Leader while others called on him to resign from the United States Senate. However, conservative Republican President George W. Bush did not believe that Lott should resign from either the Senate or the leadership post. Bush did, however, award Lott by appointing him to serve as emcee of his second Inaugural. Eventually, Lott was forced to step down from the leadership post that placed him in the line of succession to the presidency because of public pressure but would later return to become the third ranking Republican in the U.S. Senate. Despite Bush's claims of a compassionate conservatism and a Big Tent, this episode illustrated the conservative movement in the United States still harbors and protects white supremacist elements in their midst.

If contemporary conservatives were as compassionate as President Bush claimed them to be there would have been an immediate effort on the right to address Senator Lott's overtly racist statements and sanction him. Instead, President Bush and other conservatives awarded and protected Lott. Conservatism's history in America, as established in the preceding paragraphs, has been focused on protecting the advantages gained by whites as a result of the era of Jim Crow segregation without regard to whether the laws and rules of society are applied equally and rationally to all persons within this country. The lack of compassion demonstrated by conservatives in response to Trent Lott's clearly racist diatribe pales in comparison to how conservatives handle the symbols of hate.

Having compassion for one's fellow man is usually exemplified by understanding that your actions hurt others and usually results in a person not engaging in the hurtful action again regardless of whether you have a right to engage in those actions. Instead, conservatives directly engage in conduct that is divisive, immoral, evil, and cruel as it relates to the Confederate Battle flag. In particular, southern conservatives continue to argue that the Confederate Battle flag represents heritage not hatred and as such it should be freely flown on state capitol domes all across the south in honor of those lost in the fight to save the confederacy. Now is the time that southern conservatives face historical reality.

While the Stars and Bars were used by Confederate military forces during the Civil War, the Ku Klux Klan used the Confederate Battle flag to terrorize (i.e. lynching, murder, arson, etc.) the newly Freedmen of the south from the end of the Civil War to the end of the Reconstruction era and the flag came to represent the terror of those evil "Night Riders." When southern African Americans saw that flag it meant that their property would be destroyed and/or they would be beaten or even murdered. With the help of some Reconstruction era congressional enactments, in fact, the flag nearly entirely disappeared from the American scene after the federal government stamped out the early remnants of the KKK's terrorist resistance.

Even when the KKK had its resurgence during the early 1900s the terrorist organization did not revive the Stars and Bars but instead chose to use the Stars and Stripes as their official banner because even white Americans knew that the Confederate Battle flag was a symbol of treason and rebellion. It is fair to say that the Stars and Bars ranks right up there with the Nazi Swastika in its infamy and notoriety. Nevertheless, the Confederate Battle emblem did not disappear forever. As the Civil Rights movement heated up in the late 1940s and early 1950s, the white supremacist flag became increasingly present at KKK rallies as southern whites plotted how to keep control of their nigger problem as well as used on their night rides to African Americans' homes. However, one seminal event propelled the flag back onto the national stage.

The U.S. Supreme Court's decision <u>Brown v. Board</u>, discussed earlier, directly led to the reemergence of the old Confederate banner. Southern states from the eastern seaboard to the Gulf of Mexico began flying the Confederate Battle flag in protests of what they believed to be the Court's overstepping. Without this history it would be easy to see how someone could argue that the flag represents heritage not hatred. However, the United States has a well-documented history of the use of this flag to terrorize African Americans. History supports the proposition that African Americans' general negative sentiments about the Stars and Bars are well founded and rational. Based on that history, the Confederate Battle flag represents white supremacy. Even without the post-Civil War actions of KKK terrorists, history also supports the proposition that the Civil War and the rise of the Confederacy was about the southern states' specific rights to continue slavery despite southern conservatives arguing that the Civil War was fought over the general, abstract states' rights issue.

A cursory reading of the history of the Confederacy would reveal that the Confederacy was built on the issue of slavery; the rights of certain people to buy, sell, and own other people. The issue of slavery was so intertwined with the south, economically, politically, and socially, that it was inseparable from the abstraction of states' rights. Every major issue affecting the relationship between the south and the federal government revolved around slavery. Whether you are talking about the compromises that southern states negotiated into the U.S. Constitution on slavery that were addressed earlier, the Missouri Compromise, the Kansas-Nebraska Act, Bloody Kansas, the founding of the single issue (i.e. abolition) Republican Party,[88] or the presidential election of 1860, slavery was central to the events leading up to the founding of the Confederacy.

Indeed, in nearly every speech made by Confederate Vice President Alexander Stephens about Abraham Lincoln and the Union in the lead up to the Civil War, Stephens assailed Lincoln and abolitionists for trying to destroy the white race through race-mixing. Specifically, Stephens attacked Lincoln for allegedly wanting to defile white womanhood by allowing Black men to get

---

[88] The Republican Party was founded in the early 1850s by abolitionists. In 1856, John C. Fremont was their first presidential candidate who was defeated by Democrat James Buchanan. I am willing to bet that Lincoln is rolling in his grave when he sees how conservatives have destroyed the Republican Party by making it look like the old southern Democrats and Whigs of his day.

their hands on white women and denouncing the notion of racial equality. In his Cornerstone Speech delivered at Savannah, Georgia on March 21, 1861, Stephens declared that abolitionists ideas of the equality of the races were false because it violated God's law as African Americans were intended to be subordinate to the white race because of their natural inferiority. The history of the Confederacy itself condemns the Confederate Battle flag to the pages of history reserved for racism and hatred. Because the history of the Confederacy as an institution was so racist, the symbols of the Confederacy carry with them that same tarnished history. The Confederate Battle flag does represent heritage; a heritage of hatred. To deny that is to deny history and reason. Thus, the Confederacy and the Confederate Battle Flag have been undeniably tied to white supremacy and repression in America.

However, conservative indifference to, and lack of compassion for, African Americans' views of the flag persists to this day and is largely responsible for the way most African Americans view conservatives. An example of this indifference occurred in the 2000 presidential campaign. Then conservative Republican presidential candidate George W. Bush refused to condemn the flying of the Confederate Battle Flag over the South Carolina State Capitol during the 2000 presidential primary. Instead, Bush chose to say that it was a state issue withholding any personal opinion of his own even when pressed by the media because he feared losing the votes of white supremacist. When one fails to raise his voice in opposition to injustice, that failure makes the silent person just as guilty as the wrongdoer. Bush's silence is an endorsement of continued white supremacy.

Contemporarily, white Americans see Al Qaeda as the greatest threat to America's existence in history despite their only being one incident on American soil in which a few thousand were directly impacted. White supremacy has had a far larger adverse impact on the United States. Here is a brief catalog of the adverse impact. First, the Civil War nearly destroyed America at the cost of almost 700,000 lives in the six year campaign to end the racist institution of slavery. Next, Jim Crow segregation laws separated the nation into two groups—first class and second class citizens—that caused tremendous generational poverty and, even more importantly, resigned millions of African Americans to a belief that they will always be subjected to racially biased treatment in employment, education, and housing despite the statutory changes gained in the 1960s.[89] During the Civil Rights Movement, moreover, hundreds of persons, prominent and not, were assassinated for trying to advance those ideals promised to all Americans in the Constitution. Riots took place in America's major cities; some led by whites others by African Americans. The struggle to end white supremacy in America has been and is the greatest threat America faces despite Al Qaeda's heinous attack on September 11. In reality, it threatens the very integrity, unity, and strength of America.

Nevertheless, the federal government has not engaged in any campaign to eradicate this irrational and virulent ideology. Where are the efforts to extinguish right-wing white supremacy in the form of the KKK, Aryan Nations, and militias that threaten to start a racial holy war in America? Instead, for much of the second half of the twentieth century the federal government engaged in an all-out campaign to destroy the ideology of Communism internationally. Armed white supremacists run around America's forests uninhibited preparing for an alleged United Nations invasion or some other supposed "attack on America." Timothy McVeigh and Terry Nichols as well as their white supremacist brethren are no different than Osama bin Laden and Al Qaeda. They both engaged in campaigns of death and destruction against America. They both want to destroy America. One of the groups has a huge advantage over the other; the white supremacists are already within the United States numbering in the tens of thousands. As such the government should focus as much, if not more, energy and resources on ending white supremacist group's reign of terror in America as they do focusing on Al Qaeda, Communism, and whatever other isms they plan to address.

Despite the inaction by a conservative-dominated government, progressives and liberals initially attempted to address the ills caused by the generational white supremacy that had beset so much of the United States. One of the tools used to address this extensive problem was affirmative action. Progressives and liberals intended to use affirmative action to open up areas traditionally accessible only to white Americans. This included colleges and universities, unions, certain types of employment, and public contracting. Essentially, the goal was to extend access to arenas that could facilitate the rise of African Americans from

---

[89] This is perhaps the greatest victory for white supremacy—that millions of African Americans have given up. My own family carries this erroneous belief. Arguing the ridiculousness of this position is difficult to do with people who have little or no exposure to the opportunities available to them.

poverty and second class citizenship to prosperity and full citizenship.

Progressives and liberals understood that it was because of deep-seated racial bias that African Americans had been excluded from many areas of society and that the only real way to address these evils of this past and continuing racial discrimination was to open up those areas. For example, while in the past African Americans were not permitted to attend many colleges or universities simply because of the color of their skin, progressives and liberals thought that qualified African Americans should be given access to those very institutions to break the cycle of exclusion as well as allow qualified African Americans to pursue their hopes and dreams just as white Americans had been since the beginning of the United States. An additional benefit would be that African Americans would develop a broad class of professionals (physicians, accountants, attorneys, etc.).

Conservatives call affirmative action reverse discrimination. They argue that it wrongfully discriminates against white Americans, in particular white men, to benefit people of color. Their position is that the civil rights legislation that passed in the 1960s effectively made all Americans equal and because of that, there is no need for further redress. In a perfect world, they would be right but we do not live in a place called Perfect World. In reality, affirmative action is intended to remedy the lingering effects of past discrimination because simply making discrimination unlawful did not automatically put African Americans and other people of color on equal footing with white Americans. Jim Crow segregation created a large underclass of African Americans that were trapped in nearly inescapable poverty excluding the few exceptions like Madame C.J. Walker.

Despite court orders under the new federal anti-discrimination legislation, some employers continued to exclude African Americans from the workforce. The case in point is the Alabama State Troopers. In 1972, the U.S. District Court for the Middle District of the Alabama ordered the state Department of Public Safety to promote one qualified African American candidate for every white candidate.[90] Even after being ordered to promote qualified African Americans, the law enforcement organization continued to exclude African Americans from its upper ranks. Under the conservative Reagan Administration and despite the Alabama State Troopers' long history of racial discrimination

---

[90] U.S.A. v. Paradise, 480 U.S. 149 (1987).

directed toward African American applicants, the United States appealed the constitutionality of the federal court's order alleging it was a violation of the Fourteenth Amendment's Equal Protection Clause. The program established by the federal court was an affirmative action program designed to remedy the effects of past and ongoing discrimination. In fact, in this case and other cases just like it, the courts have established affirmative action programs to address this very resistance. This resistance and deeply ingrained attitude of exclusion is the focus of affirmative action.

In the aftermath of the 1960s civil rights legislation, African Americans and others began to assess the status of the Black community. What they found was that African Americans as compared to whites had lower high school and college graduation levels, had rising crime rates, lived in poorer communities with more substandard housing, had few professionals (i.e. dentists, doctors, attorneys, etc.), received a lower standard of medical care, and a host of other problems. Many historians, sociologists, and others linked these deficiencies to the effects of about 100 years of Jim Crow segregation (1876-late 1960s/early 1970s). In his *Letter from Birmingham Jail*, Dr. Martin Luther King pointed out that some African Americans were giving up altogether and resigning themselves to their positions in life.[91] During this time, white Americans were allowed to freely pursue their hopes and dreams while African Americans were forced to sit on the sidelines rather than be allowed to play the game the same as white Americans. Though African Americans had been set free physically in 1865, they were not allowed to participate in the great experiment that was America.

In America's institutions of higher learning, African Americans were routinely denied entry to public and private colleges and universities, which made it extremely difficult for African Americans to develop a robust middle class and professional class. Instead, state's created colleges and universities that were exclusively for African Americans so that they would not have to admit Blacks to the traditionally white institutions as exemplified when Alabama created Alabama State University and Alabama Agricultural & Mechanical University so that Blacks would not have to be admitted to the University of Alabama or Auburn University.

African Americans also created their own private colleges

---

[91] See Martin Luther King Jr., "Letter From Birmingham Jail," *Why We Can't Wait*, (New York: Mentor of the Penguin Group, 1964), 86-88.

and universities so that they could counterbalance the effects of the exclusion of so many African Americans from other institutions and the poor funding provided to the state-supported black colleges and universities but even they had limited space available. A few examples of these private schools are Morehouse College, Spelman College, Howard University, and Clark Atlanta University.[92] Even these measures were not enough to counter the effects of the broad exclusion from Yale University, the University of Alabama, and the numerous other private and public colleges and universities that excluded African Americans as these schools were often on the cutting edge in the professional fields. Many deserving and capable African Americans were prevented from achieving their maximum potential by Jim Crow segregation.

Despite continued discrimination and the lingering effects of Jim Crow, conservatives still attack affirmative action as unwarranted. In fact, almost immediately after affirmative action programs were put into place, conservatives attacked them. The first salvo in the attack came in Bakke v. Regents of University of California, 438 U.S. 265 (1978). Bakke, a white male medical school applicant, sued the University of California medical school for setting aside a specified number of seats for people of color only; this is called a quota. The U.S. Supreme Court agreed with Bakke holding the UC plan an unconstitutional violation of the equal protection clause of the Fourteenth Amendment because it set aside seats based on race (i.e. a quota). Conservatives won the first of many battles to come on the issue of whether race should be a factor in public university admissions. Winning the battle to outlaw quotas was not enough for conservatives. Their ultimate goal was to remove all consideration of race from postsecondary admissions decisions despite their ilk having used it for so long to exclude African Americans.

The University of Michigan would become the next battlefield in the conservative's war on affirmative action. Specifically, Michigan's undergraduate and law school's admission plans would come under attack next. Like most colleges and universities in America, Michigan's undergraduate program used a mix of objective (i.e. GPA and SAT scores) and subjective factors (i.e. personal essay, instate residency, strength of high school, underrepresented minorities, socioeconomic background, alumni [legacy] relationship, and several other categories) to decide which

---

[92] White Catholic nuns created Xavier University in New Orleans to educate African Americans.

students were admitted or not.[93] Both the objective and subjective factors were combined into a Selection Index that categorized students as "admit," "admit or postpone," "postpone or admit," "delay or postpone," and "delay or reject" with a range of points assigned to each category. Underrepresented minorities received 20 points toward the categorization.

Major universities like the University of Michigan create complex admissions procedures to ensure that the student body is diverse so that students get the benefit of learning not only about the subjects that professors lecture about but also get exposure to different points of view from people with different backgrounds as it relates to those subjects. Additionally, GPAs and SAT scores do not take into account the whole person and are not the exact in showing the likelihood of a person's success in an academic setting. The University of Michigan's undergraduate program wanted a "critical mass" of underrepresented minority students on its campus so as to avoid the isolation that prevents minority students from actively participating in classroom discussions and the like. Nevertheless, the white applicants prevailed in the undergraduate case because the Court, while admitting there was no quota system in place, did not like the assigning of points to the subjective factors since some factors were weighted more heavily than others were. Again, conservatives won another battle but they would lose the war.

The Court upheld the law school admissions program finding the goal of student body diversity a compelling state interest and that it was narrowly tailored even though race was used a factor in the admissions process.[94] The law school took into account a combination of the undergraduate grade point average and LSAT score and used a similar set of subjective factors but the subjective factors were not assigned points but instead were considered as plus factors. The Court thought that for the purposes of student body diversity race could be considered a plus factor among the many other subjective factors that the law school considered to admit students on an individualized basis. Thus, voluntary affirmative action programs in higher education were spared so long as the universities do not assign a point value to the factors they consider and individually weigh each student's application. After having lost the war, conservatives continued their opposition to affirmative action because they want to create

---

[93] Gratz v. Bollinger, 539 U.S. 244 (2003).
[94] Grutter v. Bollinger, 539 U.S. 306 (2003).

mythical colorblind society where everything is based on merit despite America's past of white supremacist favoritism.

According to conservatives, the colorblind society they dream of is one where individuals' hard work and achievements are paramount. This is a great aspiration but it cannot happen so long as racism exists, which is a huge disadvantage to people of color because they have to work harder to be treated equally and get ahead. Additionally, the conservative's position on affirmative action presupposes that America once was equal when in fact it was the very opposite as women and people of color were excluded from numerous segments of society that had become the exclusive bastions of white men. The list is extensive and they include medicine, law, engineering, and numerous others. While some of these professions have since opened up to people of color the historic exclusion continues to have long-term effects as the number of people of color in the fields are still below proportionate population levels and the upper echelons of these professions are still dominated by white Americans.

Furthermore, conservative opposition to affirmative action is like the rapist asking his victim why she now wants restorative justice. When the rapist is caught and the victim demands justice, the rapist often is surprised to see that the victim wants justice for the atrocity committed against her. The rapist often believes he has done nothing wrong and actually believes that the victim wanted it to happen. Remember, in the pre-Civil War era America, many white Americans believed that African Americans were intended by God to be slaves because they lacked the faculties for anything else just as white Americans believed that God intended African Americans and white society to be separate throughout much of America's Jim Crow segregation period. The conservative is like the rapist in that he opposes justice for the people of color of the United States; the conservative opposes restoring equality in a society historically built on inequality.

It is obvious that the opponents of affirmative action are not ready to accept America's role in the forced segregation and oppression of African Americans. However, it is very clear that African Americans are ready to forgive and move on. African American's willingness to move on and heal was best exemplified by what happened in Alabama in the lead up to the 1982 gubernatorial election.[95] Everyone remembers or has heard of

---

[95] See *The NewsHour with Jim Lehrer Transcript*, The Public Broadcasting Station, September 14, 1998, http://www.pbs.org/newshour/bb/remember/july-

Alabama's conservative Democratic Governor George C. Wallace's infamous declaration while standing in a schoolhouse door that he would not allow any African American children to attend the same school as white children. Wallace gained a reputation as a nigger-hating segregationist. After nearly being killed by an assassin during 1972's presidential campaign and seeking the redemption from his Savior, Wallace decided that he also needed to seek the forgiveness of Black Alabamians. After having sincerely, many believed, apologized in 1976 to Black Alabamians for all of the pain he caused them during that period of his life, Governor Wallace received a large percentage of the African American vote during the 1982 gubernatorial election. Once a staunch segregationist who African Americans believed hated them, Wallace recognized the error in his past deeds and apologized for his role in hindering the struggle for equal rights and Black Alabamians accepted his apology by turning out to cast their votes for this changed man.

African Americans have always wanted a simple acknowledgement from white America of the suffering that they have historically suffered. Instead, conservatives try to make comparisons between white supremacy directed toward African Americans to discrimination that Irish and Italian immigrants faced when they arrived in America. While the Irish and Italian immigrants faced de facto discrimination in America, they faced nothing even comparable to Jim Crow segregation. Irish and Italian immigrants could testify in open court against their attackers, Irish and Italian immigrants could live in neighborhoods with other white Americans, Irish and Italian immigrants could eat in restaurants and stay in hotels of their choosing, Irish and Italian immigrants could enter retail establishments through the front door, Irish and Italian immigrants did not face lynchings on a consistent basis, and Irish and Italian immigrants could own African Americans before the Civil War as evidenced by my family name, Malone. Trying to compare the plight of Irish and Italian immigrants to that of African Americans is stupid and racist.

Conservatives often respond by arguing that African Americans should not dwell on the past but should instead look to the future. This demonstrates the hypocrisy of conservatives. Since the World Trade Center was attacked and destroyed, conservatives have continuously called on Americans to never forget it. What makes one man's atrocity greater than another man's atrocity? Is it skin color? By comparison, Jim Crow

---

dec98/wallace_9-14.html.

segregation adversely affected far more people over a much longer period than the WTC attack as pointed out earlier. Yet, there is no government-funded monument for Emmett Till, James Chaney, Mickey Schwerner, Andrew Goodman, Medgar Evers, or a host of other civil rights martyrs murdered for wanting equality in America and whose murderers were largely allowed to return to their families and live out their lives.

There are numerous government-funded and private-funded monuments to the Confederacy. There should be a Civil Rights Memorial on the U.S. Capitol Mall in honor of all of those people, Black and White, Christian and Jew, who gave their lives in the fight for justice in the United States. Instead, huge segments of white America choose to celebrate hate in honoring the Confederacy. The measure of a person's character is his heart and open-mindedness. Based on the history of conservatism in America, conservatives have neither hearts nor minds because they ignore what has been staring them in the face for over 200 years. It is either time for the American conservative movement to either pursue the white supremacist within their ranks and purge them or accept that they represent an ideology of repression and white supremacy. When Chaney, Schwerner, Goodman, and others were being murdered because of their belief in equality Trent Lott, Strom Thurmond, and others were planning, in college and government respectively, to suppress the Civil Rights movement. If George Wallace can ask African Americans in Alabama to forgive him and African Americans in Alabama can forgive George Wallace's transgressions, conservatives should have the strength of character to admit their mistakes and atone for them as well.

CHAPTER 6: INDEPENDENT JUDICIARY: THE ATTACK ON THE LAST DEFENDER OF LIBERTY

Conservatives have launched an all-out assault on American courts for failing to advance their extremist right-wing agenda of rolling back individual rights in favor increased governmental control over Americans lives to advance their corporate agenda and protect the modern aristocracy. Their assault on the courts is couched in the language of judicial accountability and preventing judicial activism. In reality, conservatives dislike rulings from courts that have reaffirmed time-honored rights and liberties that are protected by our Constitution. For example, conservatives oppose the right to privacy that limits the government's authority to interfere in an individual's private life choices and affairs,[96] limits on government (i.e. police) authority to search and seize people and their property, the right to raise your children free of government mandated religious prayer and instruction in public schools,[97] the right to due process before being deprived of your life, liberty, or property in the case of Americans and foreign nationals (i.e. enemy combatants) accused of being members of Al Qaeda,[98] and the right to practice free speech and assembly

---

[96] Areas covered by this right to privacy include marriage, procreation, use of contraception, childrearing, and abortion.

[97] Again, despite the conservative myth told all across this country, the Supreme Court of the United States has ruled that the Constitution allows children to pray in public schools. This limited by the fact that government officials (i.e. faculty and administrators) are not allowed to lead such prayers on school time on school grounds.

[98] The Bush Administration made a huge mistake in not recognizing the Taliban soldiers as prisoners of war and granting them the protections of the Geneva Conventions. In the future, American soldiers that are captured on the battlefield

in society even if it is contrary to the majority of public opinion on an issue so controversial as the war on terror and 9-11 as illustrated by their monitoring of peace activists and organizations in the United States.

In addition to these attacks on our Constitution, conservatives have also launched a war on individuals' right to be compensated by a jury trial for their injuries as a result of corporate nonfeasance, misfeasance, and malfeasance. This is all done under the guise of tort reform. Conservatives claim that our judicial system is overrun with frivolous lawsuits when in fact there are some business enterprises that put products on the market knowing full well that the product poses an unreasonable risk of harm to the public as shown by the E. coli spinach and Chinese lead toy scares of 2007. Even more recently Americans have been exposed to tainted tomatoes. In an age when Congress and state legislatures have fallen under the influence of corporate campaign donations and junkets, the only way left for the little guy to get a fair hearing of his or her grievances and injuries is through the American judicial system. While Congress listens to corporate heavyweights and drafts legislation to appease them, juries listen to injured victims and grant just verdicts to compensate them for their losses. As a result of the courts protecting the public interests and not corporate interests, conservatives have called judges "activist" and began an all-out assault to dismantle and intimidate American jurists.

Oftentimes, these attacks have been accompanied with threats of retribution. Some of the threats have included dismantling entire federal circuits and de-funding federal judicial operations.[99] Individual conservatives such as Pat Robertson, Jerry Falwell, former Senator Rick Santorum (R-PA), and former House Majority Leader Tom DeLay (R-TX) have also threatened judges. These attacks create the unfounded perception among the public that American judges are all biased, unfair, or incompetent. This perception has been used by extremists to justify acts of violence against both federal and state judges. In fact, acts and threats of violence are becoming more common and more deadly as conservatives' attacks intensify. As a result of these vitriolic and vile verbal assaults, the number of threats and acts of violence against our jurists has spiked over the last several years. Conservatives say that they never encouraged violence against any judges but their use of such callous and malicious language has been the fertilizer of the abundant harvest of threats and

---

face the threat of being denied Geneva Conventions protections from an enemy government that refuses to recognize the United States government as a legitimate government. The administration has a better argument for labeling Al Qaeda militants as "enemy combatants since they do not represent a government.
[99] This actually exemplifies the reason for the Constitution's prohibition on Congress diminishing federal judges' compensation.

violence against judges.

U.S. District Court Judge Joan H. Lefkow's husband and mother were found murdered in her Chicago home in February 2005. Initially, U.S. Marshals suspected white supremacist Matthew Hale of the murders since he had previously attempted to have Judge Lefkow murdered for ruling against him in a trademark lawsuit and is serving a 40 year federal prison term for the attempted murder of Lefkow. However, the investigation revealed that a man who had received an adverse ruling in a medical malpractice suit heard by Judge Lefkow had committed the crime. In March 2005, a man, Brian Nichols, who felt that he should not be punished for the rape and assault he allegedly committed against his former girlfriend murdered a Georgia state judge in his own courtroom. These horrific incidents are just the tip of the iceberg as the issue of the right to die only added fuel to the already blazing conflagration surrounding the American courts as conservatives stepped up their attacks.

During the Terri Schiavo legal proceedings that captured America's attention in 2004, Conservatives first attempted to get Florida's Supreme Court to force the reinsertion of Terri Schiavo's feeding tube after a Florida trial court had determined that it was Ms. Schiavo's wish, based on the testimony of her husband and her friends, that she would not want to live if she was incapable of caring for herself. Having lost that battle, conservatives, who were in control of Congress, changed federal law so that federal courts would have jurisdiction to hear the Terri Schiavo case in hopes that the federal judiciary would decide the case to the satisfaction of congressional conservatives. The problem with the actions of congressional conservatives was that the issue they were granting federal courts jurisdiction over was a matter of state law under our federal system of government.

This congressional overreaching ignited a firestorm as the vast majority of Americans, as shown in poll after poll, believed that the individual and his/her family should decide whether a person who is on artificial life support should remain hooked up to the machines that keep that person alive not the government. In an ABC News Poll released March 21, 2005, it showed that 63% supported the removal of Terri Schiavo's feeding tube and 60% opposed the Republican-controlled Congress' meddling in matters of the family.[100] Additionally, a Harris Interactive poll conducted in April revealed that 58% of the public disapproved of congressional involvement and handling of the matter.[101]

---

[100] Federal Intervention in Schiavo Case Prompts Broad Public Disapproval, copyright 2005, http://abcnews.com/pollvault.html.
[101] The Terri Schiavo Case: The Paradoxically Most U.S. Adults Approve of How Both Her Husband and Her Parents Behaved, Harris Interactive Inc. Copyright

Conservatives, who had long claimed to be defenders of liberty, appeared to be attempting to expand the power of government at the expense of the individual and his/her family so much so that government decides when and how you live and die.

After the federal courts refused to overturn the Florida state court ruling, conservatives venomously attacked the federal courts who refused to pass judgment on a matter of state law that had already been decided pursuant to Florida state law (as designed by the authors of our Constitution). Had the federal court gotten involved in this case they would have been guilty of what conservatives so long claimed had taken place in America's courts (i.e. judicial activism) only it would have been at the behest of the conservative-dominated Congress; the court would have become activist and result-oriented.

After Terri Schiavo passed away, conservatives armed themselves with microphones and began a campaign to spread the message that the federal judiciary needed to be reined in. For example, Tom DeLay said "[t]he time will come for the men responsible for this to answer for their behavior" in the wake of Schiavo's death.[102] DeLay called for a congressional investigation of what he called "an out-of-control, unaccountable judiciary that thumbed their noses at Congress and the president."[103] Some conservatives proposed impeachment and conviction while other conservatives advocated redrawing federal circuit boundaries (i.e. Ninth Circuit division plan) and limiting judicial operations by reducing funding. The overall effect of these angry threats and un-American behavior has been to lower the level of respect the citizenry has for its courts and destroy the institution designed to preserve the limitations memorialized in our Constitution that protect "we the people" from the political branches overreaching. With this lowered level of respect, federal and state judicial officers and their families have seen a marked increase in the number of threats against them, attempts to attack them, actual serious injuries, and deaths. Despite DeLay's claims of federal judges "thumbing their noses," as will be shown later, the judiciary is intended to be independent from political influence whether it comes from the Congress and the president or public opinion as the Framers of our Constitution wanted the rule of law to prevail over those considerations despite DeLay's ignorant remarks.

Returning to conservatives' efforts to reign in the federal judiciary,

---

2005, http://www.harrisinteractive.com/harris_poll/index.asp?PID=558

[102] "40 years for white supremacist," *The Seattle Times (Associated Press)*, April 7, 2005.
[103] Warren Richey, "Analysts split in assessing courts' role in Schiavo case," *The Seattle Times (The Christian Science Monitor)*, April 4, 2005.

Tony Perkins, President of the Family Research Council, stated in a taped speech, "there's more than one way to take a black robe off the bench."[104] This ominous threat tears at the basic fabric of our republic because it implies that if conservatives do not obtain the results they desire in legal proceedings they will simply cripple America's judiciary, the body Alexander Hamilton called the intermediary between the people and the political branches of government with the goal of protecting the limitations placed on government in the Constitution. However, conservatives are not concerned with protecting the Constitution. They are concerned with promoting their political agenda at all costs even in contravention of the liberties that shield the American people from government overreaching. Simply put, conservatives want to take control of the judiciary. Conservatives' actions are unprecedented in American history. Even when Democratic President Franklin Delano Roosevelt and his party had huge majorities in both houses of Congress and with the Supreme Court of the United States ruling numerous pieces of New Deal legislation unconstitutional, the congressional Democrats opposed FDR's scheme to pack the high court with justices sympathetic to his cause even though it could have benefited the party's position. Modernly, congressional conservatives have made no similar effort to resist the effort to pack the American courts with Bible wielding, corporate lackeys, who are loyal only to their political party and the almighty dollar. Conservatives either have no understanding of America's constitutional history on the issue of judicial independence or, at least, they ignore it. So I hope to shed some much needed light on the subject and how the Framers intended to keep the federal judiciary accountable as well as independent.

The first thing to be established is that the Constitution contains the principle of separation of powers, despite Tom DeLay's ignorant statement of judicial officers "thumbing noses" at Congress and presidents, as the cornerstone of preserving liberty by ensuring that not all government power rested in the control of one individual or group of individuals. To wit, the federal judiciary led by the Supreme Court of the United States is a co-equal and independent branch of government. As a co-equal and independent branch of government, the judiciary is not meant, nor should it be expected, to answer directly to the president or the Congress. Notwithstanding the appointment and impeachment processes (i.e. checks and balances), the federal judiciary does not work for the president or Congress. Nor should the judiciary bend to the popular ebbs and flows of the popular opinion. Instead, the judiciary should render its decisions based on law and reason. This is what creates a conflict between majoritarian rule

---

[104] Peter Wallstein, "Evangelical groups seek 'defunding' of judges," *The Seattle Times (Los Angeles Times)*, April 23, 2005.

(democracy) and the rule of law.

Most Americans understand how the principle of democracy works. In a democracy, the majority decides what policy and law will govern society. In a representative democracy like ours, those members of Congress chosen by the people in elections are expected to represent the will of the people by enacting policy and law consistent with the will of the people. Where Americans have less understanding is with the Rule of Law principle. When a society has a basic or fundamental law embodied in a Constitution and an elected legislature adopts a law that conflicts with that Constitution, the Constitution should take precedent to the law adopted by the legislature where the two conflict. The Framers intended that the federal judiciary walk the high wire of balancing these two competing principles. Sometimes this balancing becomes very complicated and dangerous. For example, the Supreme Court of the United States has heard several petitions from persons alleged to be enemy combatants and ruled that they have a right to challenge their detention under the federal habeas corpus statute and are entitled to due process of the law under our Constitution to determine if they are appropriately classified as enemy combatants whether they are U.S. Citizens or not. This places the Court in the precarious situation of opposing the views of those Americans who think that the U.S. government should be able to indefinitely detain these "enemy combatants." However, the Court erred on the side of protecting the Rule of Law, which will be discussed later, rather than taking a poll to determine the popular opinion.

The Framers of our Constitution envisioned and prepared for the natural tension that would exist between the competing interests of the people, as sovereigns, and the Congress and the president, as their elected representatives, by placing the appointment powers in the two political branches as a check (i.e. accountability) on the federal judiciary. Under this constitutional appointment process, the president nominates the individual the president believes to be best suited to be a federal judge and the Senate holds hearings where senators question those nominees' political leanings, judicial philosophy and temperament, as well as family background. This process allows for the political fight to take place before the judge takes the bench not while the individual is sitting on the bench where the judge should be focused on legal considerations not political considerations.

Thus, the Framers created an accountable but independent judiciary. The federal judiciary would be accountable by having the people's representatives openly scrutinize judicial nominees during the appointment process with an opportunity to approve or reject the nominees but once the judges take the bench they will be allowed to make rulings that are based on sound judgment and the rule of law (i.e. Constitution) as opposed to presidential or congressional pressure. The Framers had clear and valid reasons for not allowing the people or the political branches of government to control the federal judiciary.

Alexander Hamilton, an active convention delegate and a principal proponent for the ratification of our Constitution, believed that "[w]hen the deliberative or judicial powers are vested wholly or partly in the collective body of the people, you must expect error, confusion and instability."[105] This signaled an unwillingness by the Framers to place the judiciary under the direct control and supervision of the people. The people frequently change their focus from day-to-day, which would hinder the efficiency and stability of the American legal system as the law would become more transitory with the public's changing mood counter to the purpose of the doctrine of stare decisis of ensuring legal stability and judicial efficiency by adhering to legally sound decisions.

Another benefit of distancing the people from the federal judiciary is that the courts are free to uphold the Rule of Law. The Rule of Law ensures that the basic/fundamental law is enforced fairly and equally, not arbitrarily and capriciously, in relation to all citizens regardless of stature in society even when that basic/fundamental law is in opposition to the will of the majority. This means that Lady Justice is blind. With the Rule of Law securely entrenched, conservatives are still not satisfied that the federal judiciary is fully accountable despite the comprehensive judicial nomination process that the Framers established in our Constitution. The Framers of the Constitution placed yet another accountability check on the power of the federal judiciary by making judicial officers subject to the impeachment process. Except for the fact that the Senate has established the constitutional custom of not convicting judges under articles of impeachment related to judicial acts as will be discussed later, federal judges are fully subject to the impeachment process enumerated in the Constitution including for both illegal and unethical conduct (i.e. sitting on the bench while inebriated or failing to show up for courtroom proceedings). Here, the people's elected representatives are constitutionally charged with oversight of America's judges' ethics. The process is effective because judges who have engaged, or appeared to have engaged, in inappropriate conduct were impeached, convicted, and removed from the bench. In fact, thirteen federal judges have been impeached since 1800 as illustrated below.

---

[105] Joanne B. Freeman, editor, *Writings: Alexander Hamilton*, (New York: Literary Classics of the United States, Inc., 2001), 46.

AMERICA'S JUDICIAL IMPEACHMENTS

- John Pickering, U.S. District Court for the District of New Hampshire, impeached and convicted and removed in 1803 (mental instability and intoxication on the bench)
- Samuel Chase, Associate Justice, Supreme Court of the United States, impeached and acquitted 1805 (arbitrary and oppressive conduct)
- James H. Peck, U.S. District Court for the District of Missouri, impeached and acquitted 1831 (abuse of the contempt power)
- West H. Humphreys, U.S. District Court for the Middle, Eastern, and Western Districts of Tennessee, impeached and convicted and removed 1862 (refusing to hold court and waging war against the United States)
- Mark H. Delahay, U.S. District Court for the District of Kansas, impeached and resigned 1873 (intoxication on the bench)
- Charles Swayne, U.S. District Court for the Northern District of Florida, impeached and acquitted 1905 (abuse of contempt power and other misuses of office)
- Robert W. Archbald, U.S. Commerce Court, impeached and convicted and removed 1913 (improper business relationship with litigants)
- George W. English, U.S. District Court for the Eastern District of Illinois, impeached and resigned 1926 (abuse of power)
- Harold Louderback, U.S. District Court for the Northern District of California, impeached and acquitted 1933 (favoritism in appointing bankruptcy receivers)
- Halsted L. Ritter, U.S. District Court for the Southern District of Florida, impeached and convicted and removed 1936 (favoritism in appointing bankruptcy receivers and practicing law while sitting as a judge)
- Harry E. Claiborne, U.S. District Court for the District of Nevada, impeached and convicted and removed 1986 (income tax evasion and remaining on the bench following a criminal conviction)
- Alcee L. Hastings, U.S. District Court for the Southern District of Florida, impeached and convicted and removed 1989 (perjury and conspiring to solicit a bribe)
- Walter L. Nixon, U.S. District Court for the Southern District of Mississippi, impeached and convicted and removed 1989 (perjury before a federal grand jury)

The impeachment process is a clear way for Congress to regulate the improper conduct of federal judges and has been shown to be effective.

Significantly, the impeachment process does not extend to federal judges' rulings and decisions to the chagrin of conservatives. Conservatives advocate the removal of judges whose decisions are unpopular or do not advance the conservative worldview. They argue that the current system is broken and that the federal judiciary is operating with impunity by disregarding the Constitution and the will of the people. There are numerous problems with the conservative understanding of our judicial system.

First, this position is counter to the Rule of Law, discussed previously, because the legal system goes from being logical and sound to one that is arbitrary and capricious if Congress removes judges simply because the decision of the judge is unpopular. Secondly, the U.S. Senate established a constitutional custom of not removing judges for their judicial acts in 1803 when the U.S. Senate refused to convict Associate Justice Chase on impeachment charges of being arbitrary and oppressive on the bench. While this precedent setting action preserved the independence of the federal judiciary, the Senate has not hesitated to hold judges accountable for non-judicial conduct, both unlawful and unethical, such as being intoxicated on the bench, committing perjury, practicing law while on the bench, violating the criminal law, or having improper business relationships with litigants; thus judges are removed who are a danger to the proper operation of the federal judiciary.[106] Thirdly, if the overwhelming majority of Americans disagree with a federal judicial ruling interpreting the Constitution the Framers built a process into the Constitution to lawfully and deliberatively allow the people to change the Constitution by amendment. The people and their representatives have not been hesitant in amending the Constitution when it was in their best interest to do so. The Constitution has been amended six times by the people in response to unpopular Supreme Court decisions to ensure that it met with their beliefs and desires as illustrated below.

---

[106] Even though most constitutional law scholars recognize the grave error of the Dred Scott decision and Plessy v. Ferguson, even those U.S. Supreme Court justices should not have been subject to the impeachment process for those judicial acts regardless of their inherently flawed nature.

Supreme Court Opinion	**Amendment Changing the Court's Ruling**
Chisholm v. Georgia[107]	11th Amendment (1798): State's immune from suits by persons from other states
Scott v. Sanford[108]	14th Amendment (1868): Citizenship of those born in U.S., equal protection, due process
Pollock v. Farmers' Loan and Trust Co.[109]	16th Amendment (1913): Income Tax
Minor v. Happersett[110]	19th Amendment (1920): Women's Voting 23rd Amendment (1961): DC Presidential electors
Breedlove v. Suttles[111]	24th Amendment (1964): Poll Tax
Oregon v. Mitchell[112]	26th Amendment (1971): Voting Age 18

Each of these amendments was in direct response to some U.S. Supreme Court decision that dissatisfied a broad swath of the American populace so much so that they believed our basic law, the Constitution, needed to be amended. This accounts for fully 35% of the constitutional amendments since the adoption of the Bill of Rights. Conservative arguments that "the will of the people" is thwarted when judges make rulings that are unpopular simply do not hold water. On the contrary, the will of the people ultimately prevails through the enforcement of their Constitution and when the Constitution is amended to satisfy their expectations of government. Despite this constitutional framework operating without a hitch for much of America's existence, conservatives prefer to usurp this constitutional dispute resolution process in favor of legislative enactments that clearly violate the Constitution which undermines the Rule of Law. That is to say, conservatives prefer the arbitrary to the sound, the capricious to the logical.

Even when the majority of the public supports it, the legislative branch cannot be allowed to adopt legislation in contravention of the Constitution. For example, conservatives would like to ban flag burning by congressional enactment despite the federal judiciary finding that such activity is expressive conduct protected by the Free Speech Clause of the

---

[107] 2 U.S. 419 (1793).
[108] 60 U.S. 393 (1857).
[109] 157 U.S. 429 (1895).
[110] 88 U.S. 162 (1874).
[111] 302 U.S. 277 (1937).
[112] 400 U.S. 112 (1970).

First Amendment to the Constitution of the United States. The Constitution not only places limits on government but it also places limits on the will of the majority by protecting the rights of the minority. The Framers, the anti-democrats they were, did not wish to allow majority rule to advance unchecked. Instead, they wanted to establish a society where law and reason prevailed over the passions of the masses. Alexander Hamilton wanted to ensure that the public understood that

> the right of the people to alter or abolish the established constitution whenever they find it inconsistent with their happiness exists without a doubt; yet it is not to be inferred from this principle, that the representatives of the people, whenever a momentary inclination happens to lay hold of a majority of their constituents incompatible with the provisions in the existing constitution, would on that account be justifiable in a violation of those provisions; Until the people have by some solemn and authoritative act [i.e. amendment] anulled or changed the established form, it is binding upon themselves collectively, as well as individually.[113]

The will of the people, as far as the Framers were concerned, is embodied in the Constitution.[114] It is the people who through their ratifying conventions and, later, elected state legislatures adopted the Constitution and its now twenty-seven amendments respectively. Thus, judicial adherence to this basic/fundamental law represents the enforcement of "the will of the people." The people may, at any time, alter that basic/fundamental law embodied in the Constitution through the amendment process. Conservatives have attempted to confuse the issues by portraying the judiciary as out of touch with the will of the people. In fact, conservatives are out of touch with the people. They are out of touch because they want to expand government power at the expense of the people's liberty. Conservatives are of the mindset that if Congress decides to ban flag burning, require prayer in public schools, or fund religious organizations to carry out economic aid programs that Congress should be the judge of whether it is acting within the confines of the Constitution in direct contravention of the Framers' intent.

As the Constitution imposes limitations on government power, someone or somebody must have responsibility for ensuring that these limitations are enforced. Should the Congress and/or the president be

---

[113] Freeman, *Writings: Alexander Hamilton*, 425.
[114] See Wills, *The Federalist Papers*, 395-396.

permitted to determine for themselves the extent of their constitutional authority? The Framers of the Constitution rejected both political branches of government as repositories of this great responsibility and opted for the federal judiciary. They immediately recognized that the federal judiciary would not be able to carry out this prestigious and solemn obligation if Congress and the president controlled the courts. The Framers realized that the Congress and office of the presidency were far and away the stronger of the branches of government. Because of the disparity in power between the federal judiciary and the other two branches of government, "[the federal courts are] in continual jeopardy of being overpowered, awed, or influenced by its coordinate branches."[115] In fact Alexander Hamilton weighed the power of the three branches of government and found that

> the judiciary, from the nature of its functions, will always be the least dangerous to the political rights of the constitution; because it will be least in a capacity to annoy or injure them…The judiciary…has no influence over either the sword or the purse, no direction either of the strength or of the wealth of the society, and can take no active resolution whatever. It may truly be said to have neither FORCE nor WILL, but merely judgment; and must ultimately depend upon the aid of the executive arm even for the efficacy of its judgments. This simple view of the matter suggests several important consequences. It proves incontestibly that the judiciary is beyond comparison the weakest of the three departments of power; that it can never attack with success either of the other two; and that all possible care is requisite to enable it to defend itself against their attacks. It easily proves, that though individual oppression may now and then proceed from the courts of justice, the general liberty of the people can never be endangered from that quarter; I mean so long as the judiciary remains truly distinct from both the legislative and executive. For I agree that 'there is no liberty, if the power of judging be not separated from the legislative and executive powers.' And it proves, in the last place, that liberty can have nothing to fear from the judiciary alone, but would have everything to fear from its union with either of the other departments[116]

---

[115] Freeman, *Writings: Alexander Hamilton*, 422.
[116] Id. at 421-422.

Thus, it was settled that the judiciary required some special protection from the other branches. This protection included constitutional provisions granting federal jurists' lifetime appointments subject only to impeachment and prohibiting Congress from reducing their salaries during their service on the federal bench. These protections were intended to protect the judiciary's independence and represented the constitutionalization of the concept of judicial independence.

"The complete independence of the courts of justice is peculiarly essential in a limited constitution."[117] Specifically, it is essential as a benefit to the people and their Constitution. The Framers of the Constitution intended the shield of judicial independence to protect the people from their national government by charging the federal judiciary with the duty to enforce the limitations imposed on the political branches in the Constitution. According to Alexander Hamilton, "[T]he courts were designed to be an intermediate body between the people and the legislature, in order, among other things, to keep the latter within the limits assigned to their authority."[118] The federal judiciary is essentially the guardian of that basic/fundamental law embodied in the Constitution. As the constitutional guardian, the federal judiciary issues judgments essential to keeping the powerful Congress and president from thwarting the will of the people; the Constitution.

For example, the Constitution clearly establishes that Congress cannot pass any laws that make conduct criminal retroactively if it was not criminal when the conduct took place (ex post facto clause). As such, if Congress does enact legislation that contravenes the meaning of this constitutional provision, the federal judiciary would be expected to find that the Constitution takes precedent over this legislative provision. "Limitations of this kind [i.e. the ex post facto clause and others] can be preserved in practice in no other way than through the medium of the courts of justice; whose duty it must be to declare all acts contrary to the manifest tenor of the constitution void. Without this, all the reservations of particular rights or privileges would amount to nothing."[119]

> Laws are but dead letters without courts to expound and define their true meaning and operation. The treaties of the United States to have any force at all, must be considered as part of the law of the land. Their true import as far as respects individuals, must, like all other laws, be ascertained by judicial determinations. To

---

[117] Id. at 422.
[118] Id. at 423.
[119] Id. at 422.

produce uniformity in these determination, they ought to be submitted in the last resort, to one SUPREME TRIBUNAL.[120]

If the federal judiciary were under the control or direct supervision of the Congress, as conservatives propose it should be, the federal judiciary would be less likely to find congressional enactments unconstitutional as members of the judiciary would have to worry about satisfying the will of the Congress as opposed to adhering to the Rule of Law. This would sound the death knell for the U.S. Constitution and the end of liberty in America. In reality, it would be a return to the days of King George III.

Despite all of this clear constitutional history, conservatives continue on their drive to remake the federal judiciary. Conservatives want to overturn the last sixty years of jurisprudence that has upheld clearly established constitutional rights that had previously been ignored by the political branches of government. As the people's intermediaries, the federal judiciary has merely enforced the will of the people by declaring the following unconstitutional actions of government: (1) de jure racially segregated schools, (2) government interference in a woman's right to decide whether to have an abortion or whether to use contraceptives, (3) statute's prohibiting adults of the same sex from engaging in consensual sexual acts in private, (4) state laws requiring children to pray during the public school day, (5) laws prohibiting flag burning, interrogating and detaining criminal suspects without informing them of their constitutional rights, and (6) the death penalty's application to persons who committed their criminal offenses who were mentally retarded or who were minor children at the time of the offense. Because of these decisions and many others, the federal judiciary has come under intense scrutiny by conservatives for upholding the Rule of Law (i.e. the Constitution) and the will of the people embodied in that Rule of Law because the courts have appropriately served as a bulwark against conservative's attempts to advance their ideology at the expense of our Constitution. A couple of those aforementioned decisions drew intense vitriol and threats from conservatives because the author of the decisions chose to protect the rule of law through logic and reason rather than engage in ideological partisan politics.

Associate Justice Anthony M. Kennedy, a Reagan appointee, authored two opinions that have moved America to a more civilized and humane position on the relationship between individual liberty and government power. In Lawrence v. Texas, 539 U.S. ___ (2003), police officers were summoned to an address to investigate an alleged gun

---

[120] Id. at 249.

disturbance. When the officers arrived at the residence they noticed the door was ajar. Upon entering the residence, the officers found two men engaged in sexual conduct. Both men were arrested, charged, and convicted under Texas' anti-homosexual sodomy statute. Justice Kennedy wrote the majority opinion that struck down the statute as the Court found no government interest in regulating the private, sexual conduct of consenting adults under the Fourteenth Amendment's Due Process Clause. Religious conservatives insulted Justice Kennedy for not allowing the government to regulate this private conduct and abandoning Reagan's legacy. That was not the last time Justice Kennedy drew the ire of the religious right.

In March 2005, Justice Kennedy authored another majority opinion in Roper v. Simmons, 543 U.S. __ (2005), upholding the Missouri Supreme Court's decision that the use of the death penalty against persons who committed their criminal offenses as minors was unconstitutional under the Eighth Amendment's Cruel and Unusual Punishment Clause. Despite the Missouri Supreme Court ordering Simmons death sentence be changed to life without the possibility of parole or early release, religious conservatives angrily denounced the decision. Having received some real Christian indoctrination as a child, I understand that the principle of an eye for an eye found in the Old Testament was abandoned by Jesus Christ in favor of the more modern "turn the other cheek" principle found in the New Testament Gospels. However, it appears that many religious conservatives live in the Old Testament as opposed to follow the teachings of Jesus Christ. Notwithstanding the hypocrisy displayed by religious conservatives, religious conservatives also attacked Justice Kennedy on legal content of his decision.

In particular, conservatives like to say that Justice Kennedy relied on international law to decide the case. That is an absolute fabrication of the truth. Only after having determined that the imposition of the death penalty against persons convicted of heinous criminal offenses committed as minors was unconstitutional under U.S. law, Justice Kennedy reviewed the international status quo to see where the United States stood in comparison to the rest of the world.[121] Additionally, had Justice Kennedy used international legal standards such as treaties or customs to determine the validity of the application of the death penalty to minors; he would have

---

[121] See Roper v. Simmons, 543 U.S. 551 (2005) ("Our determination that the death penalty is disproportionate punishment for offenders under 18 finds confirmation in the stark reality that the United States is the only country in the world that continues to give official sanction to the juvenile death penalty. This reality does not become controlling, for the task of interpreting the Eighth Amendment remains our responsibility.")

been constitutionally justified.

The Constitution contemplates international law as a part of the body of U.S. law because the president is authorized to make treaties with foreign powers, the U.S. Senate is authorized to ratify those treaties, and the federal courts have subject matter jurisdiction over cases or controversies arising out of treaties. Additionally, the Constitution considers international law to be a part of the U.S. domestic law as treaties are mentioned in the Supremacy Clause in Article VI of the Constitution of the United States. Finally, the Constitution grants Congress the authority "to define and punish piracies and felonies committed on the high seas, and offenses against the law of nations."[122] This last provision is perhaps the most damning to the argument of conservatives that international law has no place in American courtrooms. In fact, the Founding Fathers considered America's laws to consist not just of our own Constitution but also include "[o]ur treaties and the laws of nations form part of the law of the land."[123] Yet again, the conservatives are out of touch with reality and history in an effort to rewrite U.S. constitutional history to benefit their twisted version of America. Thus, if Justice Kennedy had relied on international law in his legal analysis in the Roper decision it would have rested on the solid foundation of constitutional text and history. The attacks on Justice Kennedy's civil libertarian stance (i.e. pro-individual rights) and other judicial officers is simply one of the fronts in the all-out assault of conservative, nay proto-fascist, aristocrats on the hallowed U.S. Constitution's limitations on government power by discrediting the courts with trumped up allegations of unprofessionalism and bias.

The repercussions have been a barrage of violence and threats directed at the judiciary. They want the people to believe that the judiciary is not working for them. Quite to the contrary the judiciary is holding the line against an ever advancing conservative corporatist, warmongering, and religious fundamentalist's agenda. It is the federal judiciary that has turned back attempts by President George W. Bush to grasp more power that the Constitution permits (i.e. detainees and electronic eavesdropping on U.S. citizens). Most Americans are asleep on the issue of an independent judiciary and its link to protecting their liberty. Conservatives biggest fear is that the masses of Americans will wake up and see exactly how they are trying to dismantle the constitutional safeguards to our liberty in favor of more government power. Most Americans will not realize the judiciary's importance until it is too late. My hope is that this book is the wakeup call America needs.

---

[122] Constitution Article I, section 8, clause 10.
[123] Freeman, *Writings: Alexander Hamilton*, 809.

CHAPTER 7: CHANGING OUR FUTURE

Thus far this book has focused on how conservatives have historically and contemporarily posed a serious threat to the liberty of Americans and our Constitution but made very little mention of democracy even though the title of the book is *The Death of Liberty and Democracy*. The link between liberty and democracy is not complicated however it is exceedingly important. Conservatives know that by attacking the liberty of the people, that is to say the people's ability to freely live their lives, freely make their own decisions, and freely question their government and make demands of it, they will have a much easier time controlling and manipulating the people's choices through the representative democratic process. The ultimate mission of progressives and liberals is to engage in a national campaign to educate our fellow Americans about the concept of liberty and how it is essential to their democracy.

Most Americans think of "liberty" as a negative; that is to say the government cannot stop the individual from engaging in certain activities. While that is true, another even more important component of liberty is that it allows the people to control their government's actions as intended by the Framers of our Constitution, which is also supported by provisions of the U.S. Constitution and our constitutional history. An example of the former is the First Amendment which contains the free speech, free press, free assembly, and the right to petition the government clauses. While the First Amendment contains the language that the government "shall make no law," the very tenor of the amendment's provisions taken as a whole is to allow the public to comment on, and criticize, the actions of their government as well as make demands of that government. The Framers saw this republic as a participatory representative democracy where an educated people would know what government was up to and object when government acted in violation of their wishes and/or make specific demands of government to act when the people wanted it to act. Essentially, the people are the government. In Federalist No. 39, James Madison, the father of the Bill of Rights, in addressing the importance of a republic stated that:

> It is evident that no other form would be reconcileable with the genius of the people of America; with the fundamental principles of the revolution; or with that honorable determination, which animates every votary of freedom, to rest all our political experiments on the capacity of mankind for self-government.[124]

We know this notion of self-governance is extremely important to the Framers because of colonial American history and American jurisprudence.

In the Framers' historic run-ins with King George III, the chief complaint of the colonists related to taxation without representation, which is an overly simplistic way of understanding the dispute. More accurately, the Framers, many of them wanting to be loyal subjects to the Crown, wanted a voice in the decisions made by Parliament that affected the British North American colonies as well as greater autonomy to govern their own affairs on the other side of the pond. Essentially, when colonists attempted to petition the King and Parliament for redress of their grievances related to the new taxes and other royal decrees (e.g. Royal Proclamation of 1763), they were rebuffed as if they were not entitled to question the Crown or Parliament.

On several occasions, the Framers sent representatives like Benjamin Franklin to London to present their grievances directly in an effort to seek redress. Only after these numerous efforts to request relief from the established government had failed did the Framers seriously consider rebelling against the Crown. In response, King George III cracked down by arresting critics of his government, torturing individuals suspected of participating in plotting rebellion, searching homes of suspected insurgents to find weapons, and many other oppressive acts. It is this history that led to the Framers adopting the language of the First Amendment and other parts of the Constitution to ensure that the people had a way to control their government. American constitutional jurisprudence supports this historical interpretation.

The Supreme Court of the United States has identified political speech as the most protected form of speech because the inherent reason the Framers adopted the First Amendment was to allow the people the

---

[124] See Wills, *The Federalist Papers*, 189.

opportunity to freely voice their opinions about their government's actions without fear of detention, torture, or death as often was the case when the red coats arrested a person suspected of criticizing the Crown. The freedoms of assembly and to petition government are also closely related to this purpose. The Court reached this point by reviewing the Framers' writings to discern their intent and discovered the Framers had an affinity for classical liberal philosopher John Locke. Locke advanced similar notions of liberty in his many writings about the rights of the governed, which positively influenced the 1787 Philadelphia Convention and James Madison the author of the Bill of Rights.

In his Two Treatises of Government, John Locke described mankind's true natural state as being in a "state of perfect freedom" and "equality, wherein all power and jurisdiction is reciprocal, no one having more than another" that carries with it the absolute right to make one's own decisions about every aspect of one's life free from the control of others but recognizing that one cannot infringe on the rights of others. These are central themes of classical liberalism that reject any notion of monarchy, aristocracy, oligarchy, or theocracy. According to Locke, a person only gives up this "perfect freedom" and equality when that person voluntarily chooses to enter into a common form of government with another group of individuals but even that surrender of rights is limited because the people always retain the right to reject any government that portends to have the power to breach promises made to the people and/or limitations placed on its power. While this is not an all-encompassing discussion of Locke's theories of civil government, it clearly focuses you on Locke's central ideal of liberty and the rights of the people to control any government they should establish, which absolutely influenced our Founding Fathers.

What is clear in our history is that liberty is paramount for public control of political institutions. For the public to be able to successfully criticize and, thereby, control their government using their rights of free speech, assembly, and petition, the people need to have unfiltered, truthful information, which can only be obtained through a free press unconstrained by government censorship. In sum, the positive import of the concept of liberty is that by the American people receiving factual information about their government from a free press they are in a better position to comment on, criticize the actions of, and make demands of, government when exercising their free speech, assembly, and petitioning rights. Thus, the Framers' dreams of a representative democracy in which an active and educated citizenry are fully engaged would be realized.

Elite conservatives (i.e. the landed and moneyed aristocracy like the Bushes, the Forbeses, etc.) are fully aware of the Framers reasons for enshrining these important civil liberties in the Constitution, but they are also fully aware that they would not be able to maintain control of an informed, educated, and active people, which explains why they have engaged in a campaign of obfuscating America's history. Why have they done this?

Elite conservatives want to protect their continued dominance of the political, economic, and social arena of the United States by their class. When I say elite conservatives I am referring to those who are in the American aristocracy because the average American who denominates himself conservative is unaware of this history and largely unmotivated to learn anything else because they are comfortable with the status quo of well-woven lies they have been fed by the elite conservatives; this is the docility that elite conservatives have wanted to create in the populace.

Elite conservatives chastise people on the left of the political spectrum for "statements" that denounce the evils of class warfare while elite conservatives are engaged in all out economic genocide against the middle class and the working class a.k.a. blue collar workers. With the middle class and working class of the Red States distracted by the usual conservative themes addressing religion, firearms, and gay rights, the elite conservatives use their money to control Congress and the president of the United States. Essentially, conservatives have convinced millions in the Red States to cede control of their government to corporate interests without them even realizing it.

President Ronald Reagan once remarked that the scariest words that a person could ever hear were "I am from the government and I am here to help you." Notwithstanding the fact that many Red Staters feel this way, the earlier chapters clearly demonstrate how elite conservatives successfully convinced millions of Americans that their government is their enemy while the same elite conservatives used the government to benefit their friends in corporate America thereby making the government the friends of the corporate elite.

Returning to the mission of progressives and liberals, it is more important to explain to Americans that they are the government and that the allegedly sacred private sector are their opponents. However, the conservative movement's propaganda for the last fifty years has created in the public a trust of corporate America and private enterprise. Many Americans have learned over the last 8 years that their trust has been sorely misplaced as demonstrated by rampant falsification of financial records as illustrated by Arthur Anderson-Enron, MCI Worldcom, Qwest, Adelphia, and nearly 200 other corporate scandals at the start of the new millennium and the collapse of major U.S. financial institutions in 2008 because of unregulated lending of money by financial institutions to people who could not afford to repay those loans in their speculative efforts to make money.

History has shown Americans yet again that unregulated capitalism is unworkable because people in positions of power will do almost anything for a few more dollars. This is not intended to suggest that capitalism is a failure; it is only intended to demonstrate the capitalism needs regulation or the taxpayers will be asked to bailout American corporations that take unnecessary speculative risks that threaten the economic security of everyone.

Yet, conservatives continue to want Americans to cede control of their government to corporations despite the fact that laissez faire capitalism is a danger to the many. Conservatives persist in their desire to sell off, or contract out, traditional government services to private industry. Under the Bush Administration, conservatives have been largely successful in their move toward this type of government. Everything from providing taxpayer money to so called faith-based programs that provide *services* to contracting out the protection of American ambassadors and other diplomats to private security firms to creating a prescription drug program for senior citizens designed wholly to protect the pharmaceutical giants and not the American taxpayer, the Bush Administration began in earnest to divide the American government into slices to be doled out to corporations piece by piece. The federal government is not the only place where government services are being privatized at an alarming rate.

States and local governments all across America are privatizing public entities as the solution to all problems. States are letting the Corrections Corporation of America run their prisons. Cities and water districts are allowing private firms to provide the extremely important water quality testing for the public's all important water supply without learning the lessons of Walkerton, Ontario where many individuals were sickened and some died from tainted water when a private firm failed to carry out its obligation to test the local water supply as agreed. Much of these privatization schemes are done at the expense of American worker safety and the taxpayer. For example, a prison facility run by the Corrections Corporation of America sustained severe damage and many inmates and correctional staff suffered serious injuries in a riot that occurred in Olney Springs, Colorado on July 20, 2004. This was not the first or the last time that a privately run prison suffered from rioting inmates resulting in losses in the hundreds of thousands of dollars to state taxpayers. Nevertheless, the corporate-owned "liberal media's" failure to investigate this and many other abuses of the taxpayers' trust only proves the inter-corporate relationships that cross industry lines from media to prisons to water quality management and so on and so forth as scandal after scandal is swept under the rug by the national "liberal media."

There is a clear record of corporate America taking advantage of Americans and an even clearer record of government providing services like fire, police, military, and other public services relatively well not to mention the success of the President Roosevelt's New Deal for reshaping America and creating the Great American Middle Class of the 1950s. Even more damaging to the conservative's argument is their hypocrisy of on the one hand preaching that the government can do nothing right, while on the other hand using the government to assist their conservative allies in corporate America in achieving the spread of their fanatical brand of fascistic corporatism throughout the globe and getting special legislation for subsidies and taxes adopted on a regular basis.

If you were to talk to an American who lived in the Depression Era, their perspective on government is drastically different from today's American. Americans in that era saw the collapse of laissez faire (unregulated) capitalism under the weight of corporate corruption and greed. It was only under the tutelage of President Franklin Delano Roosevelt, as previously mentioned, that America slowly climbed out of the Depression and created the largest middle class in American history. However, conservatives, by rewriting history, have successfully convinced millions that government should operate like private industry with an eye toward efficiency only and that the large post-World War II middle class was the result of corporations not the major redistribution of wealth that was at the center of the New Deal.

There are two problems with the notion that government should operate like business: (1) "efficiency" in private industry means profit, which is not the basis for providing public services, the goal of government is to provide the service to the broadest number of people effectively, and (2) private industry has been proven over the last decade to be more corrupt than ever as illustrated in the Adelphia, Enron, MCI WorldCom, HealthSouth, and nearly 200 other major American corporations overstating their earnings to bilk millions of Americans out of their pensions and other investments in a similar fashion as occurred in the stock market crash that led to the Depression and 25% unemployment of 1933. So the conservative plan to privatize everything falls flat on its face as proven by history; they will never learn from history.

Corporations do not need an advocate in government. They have billions of dollars at their disposal to pay lobbyists to carry their interests to members of Congress. It is the people who need an advocate in government. In fact, government should serve the people not corporate America's agenda. The only way we as Americans can truly exercise our control over government and get it to serve our interests is by taking a direct and active role in our government. Simply voting is not good enough. We have to take a critical eye to any government policy decisions that serve interests other than our interests. This requires us to ask questions about proposed laws in our national, state, and local legislative assemblies. In order for us to ask the right questions we need the "liberal media" to provide use with critical information about government and its ties to corporate America. In fact, we need our media to provide us with more information about the operation of our government and less information about "Brangelina" or some celebrity running shirtless on the beach. Once the media provides us with this information we can actually exercise our liberty by exercising the control we are constitutionally entitled to over our government.

In Europe, people take to the streets in massive protests when government plans to make a decision that the masses oppose and are often successful. For example, former French President Sarkozy wanted to reform the 35 hour work week. In response, several hundred thousand French citizens took to the streets in protest forcing the government to back down. Some Americans see protesting as a nuisance because it slows down traffic and ineffective in getting any results modernly making it easy for conservatives to, for example, say that not many Americans were against the war in Iraq. Lending support to that line of thought, the "liberal media" failed to air any coverage of large street protests in the lead up to the war for fear of retribution from their conservative corporate executives because perhaps airing such footage might have caused some Americans to think twice about going to war. The point here is we need support from the press to exercise our control.

The press should be providing Americans with information. Information about the operations of government. Sometimes that means that the press would have to burn their sources. That is to say, name the source who leaked a piece of information about a program to prove the validity of the information. However, concern over losing the source by the members of the corporate-owned press corps is used as a justification for not disclosing the identity of the source. So instead, Americans end up with the news reports of unnamed sources disclosing information with no way of following up on the information to learn if it is true or not. The real losers under this approach are the American people. Thus, corporate ownership of the press is the problem.

If the press were actually performing as it was intended, important issues would be front in center with the American people as opposed to the focus being on personalities of politicians and reporting "both sides of the story" as if there is equivalency in the arguments of both parties when one group is actually making false statements. One example of the false equivalency approach of the media is carrying the story about death panels as declared by Sarah Palin and other conservative personalities. While there is no evidence to support the position that President Obama's Affordable Care Act created any death panels, conservatives stated it as a fact over and over again saying that the president wanted to kill grandma. None of the corporate media elites challenged the assertion as false except for Rachel

Maddow and Chris Matthews. If the corporate media were actually doing their job, a litany of important issues facing our country would be at the forefront right now and the corporate-owned "liberal media" would (1) let the conservatives make their arguments for/against adopting/changing specific policies, (2) the liberals make their arguments for/against adopting/changing specific policies, and (3) investigate both sides' positions on those policies and report to the American people which side is factually accurate. It is the third piece that is currently missing from the national "liberal media" coverage. If this were taking place Americans would better informed about issues like:

- FOOD SAFETY POLICY REFORM
- DEFENSE POLICY REFORM
- EDUCATIONAL POLICY REFORM
- NATURAL RESOURCE PROTECTION
- LABOR REFORM
- ILLEGAL DRUG REFORM
- TRANSPORT INFRASTRUCTURE
- TAX POLICY REFORM
- PROVIDING ADEQUATE VETERAN ASSISTANCE
- ELECTION & VOTING REFORM

If Americans paid more attention to these issues and received factual media coverage of them rather than five hours of coverage about Paris Hilton's trip to jail, the conservative movement would falter and be forced to change or die. The solutions to the real issues facing America are not consistent with big business' agenda of maintaining control over an underpaid and overworked labor force. Some solutions will require big business to change the way it operates. Nevertheless, conservatives have cornered the market on controlling the "liberal media" and, thus, the people through fear and misinformation. The people now have to be proactive in digging up the information that will expose the lies of the right wing. Sadly, this may only occur with the faltering of the economy or some other catastrophe.

In the aftermath of the September 11 attacks, the conservatives immediately took advantage of the opportunity to roll out their agenda. The conservative Bush Administration gave billions of taxpayer dollars to contracting firms for security, services for the troops, disaster recovery plans, and a whole host of other things. The problem was that the contractors (the exalted private industry) were ripping off the taxpayers by either not completing the contracts or poorly performing the services for which they were hired.

For example, the firm the government hired to create an evacuation plan for New Orleans and southern Louisiana received the taxpayers' funds but never produced the evacuation plan as was discovered when people tried to locate it in the run-up to Hurricane Katrina making landfall. Even more damning, researchers at the Louisiana State University had already drafted a plan for evacuation that would not have cost the American taxpayer one dime but because of the Bush Administration's big business ties and its opposition to the researchers who believe that climate change was responsible for the continued erosion of the Louisiana coastline leading to more severe hurricanes the administration did not want anything to do with these researchers. Thus, conservatives have set in motion their plan to complete the turnover of our government to the corporations.

Now it is our turn to act. We have to demand that the government serve our interests and not the interests of the corporate and wealthy elite. We have to demand that the government stay out of our private affairs. If not we will become the slaves of corporate America with the government as our overseer; making sure we work our jobs with little or no benefits, not question the actions of government making us "real Americans" according to conservatives, and overspend on things we do not need amassing huge amounts of public debt with the final result that we will have spent very little time with the people we care about most because we are spending all of our time serving our corporate masters as wage slaves. Under that state of affairs their truly can be no liberty or democracy.

So what can be done to save our nation? We can recognize that the current two party system is the problem. Lobbyists for corporate interests give money to politicians like California Democratic Senator Diane Feinstein and Kentucky Republican Senator Mitch McConnell to have an influential advocate advancing funding for weapons systems, tax advantages, and a host of other goodies. This guarantees that corporate interests will be represented no matter what party is in charge. This also guarantees that decisions are not being made in the best interest of Americans. The system needs to be turned on its head. The best way to do that is a full on peaceful, democratic revolution.

First, Americans have to let go of the notion that one person can reform the system. Many liberals and progressives were massively disappointed with the presidency of Barack Obama. They expected that his mere election as president would change everything. His victory speech on the night of his election in Chicago in 2008 seemed to signal that he understood that he needed the people behind him. He made a statement that confounded some television talking heads when he said, paraphrasing here, we are the people we have been waiting for. This seemed to indicate that he knew that he needed the American people but he seemed to falter or not make any effort after that night to articulate that idea in any detail or talk to the people and ask for their direct action to get things done.

There is a tendency on the part of people in general and Americans in particular to favor strong individual leaders. That is to say, when people see a strong person among them, those people like to follow those strong leaders. Thus, in the persona of a president people see the ability of the leader to do anything. However, the truth is far from that in this country. The real power of the American government lies within the control of the Congress of the United States as President Franklin D. Roosevelt understood. Any effort to really change and save our nation has to be done through the mechanism of the Congress. The plan to give us the revolution we thought we would get under President Obama can be obtained through the Congress but not as it is currently constituted or as it will be constituted after future elections under either the Democratic Party or the Republican Party. But there is a way to take control of American's legislative body but it is by no means a simple task.

To reform American government, it will take a sustained effort of about ten years. It will take that long because of the structural impediments to massive reform that the Framers built into the American legislative system. Chief among the impediments is the U.S. Senate's continuing nature. Under the plan of the convention, senators would serve six year terms with one-third of them up for election every two years. This means that at no single election do the American voters ever elect a new senate. Instead, the body's institutional memory is protected and preserved. Why would the Framers do this? The central goal was to establish a stable republic. By having a continuous senate the legislative process wouldn't see wild political swings after each election and vast legislative changes similar to those that occur in the parliamentary system like the United Kingdom. Instead, the senate would be a calm, deliberative body that slows the legislative process down to allow for thoughtful consideration of new laws. However, this hasn't been the case recently in the American government. Instead, some senators have used the Senate as a way to deny any consideration of legislative change by simply bottling up new laws and not debating them at all with threats of filibusters (that they never actually go through with). This can all change. We have the power to make it change.

What we need to do on a massive scale is recruit about sixty to eighty million Americans to the cause of reform to (1) identify 535 Americans that they know in their community who have never held political office or sought political office that would be good reform-minded candidates for the U.S. House and Senate, (2) get each of the sixty million to contribute about $5 per person to run ads to support these candidates, and (3) adopt a legislative and constitutional amendment platform that the 535, if elected, would advance in Congress. The first thing that you are probably wondering is how would anyone accomplish such a massive task. The answer is using the internet.

The reform movement would find that the most effective means of organizing the citizenry of this large country of ours would be by establishing a website. A website would make it easy for the movement to communicate with its members and develop a consistent plan of action. On this website, you could ask the public to identify the candidates needed to represent the movement, raise the money to advertise the nominated candidates and promote the ideas, and vote for the top legislative proposals that should be promoted by of these candidates that are elected.

First, we would need the sixty to eighty million supporters to vote online for the top legislative proposals that would help improve our government for the benefit of all Americans not just Wall Street. Based on the vote of these supporters, the top twenty to thirty legislative proposals would be the focus of any elected members of the movement. In fact, there would be two votes for legislative proposals by all of the supporters. One vote that deals with government reform and another that deals with substantive legal reform to benefit American citizens. The initial focus should be on a government reform agenda. Some of the items that supporters of the movement may want to consider would consist of:

- Banning elected officials from voting on bills that they or their immediate family members have a potential conflict of interest with
- Providing easier ballot access to the third parties and independent candidates
- Eliminating the Senate's filibuster rule
- Amending the Constitution to explicitly and strongly provide for the individual right of privacy (excluding all corporate entities)
- Setup a process for publicly funded presidential debates that allow for more direct public participation
- Amending the Constitution to prohibit DNA collection from arrestees who have not been convicted
- Amending the Constitution to give Congress the authority to regulate campaign contributions
- Amending the Constitution to give the president the line-item veto for budget bills exclusively
- Amending the Constitution to require Congress to adopt a budget every single year and, if Congress fails to do so, every member of Congress will lose a day of pay for each

day beyond the start of the new fiscal year the nation goes without a new budget

After addressing the government reform agenda, then the focus can turn to any identified substantive legal changes that the movement's supporters would like to see. Some of the items may include things like:

- Banning the National Security Agency from gathering domestic electronic information
- Banning the use of drones for law enforcement and investigative purposes within the United States
- Auditing the Federal Reserve system
- Reinstating the portion of the Glass-Steagall Act that prohibited consumer banks, investment banks, and insurers from doing each other's business
- Eliminating the use of free speech zones
- Overhauling the Internal Revenue Code
- Implementing a plan to repair America's infrastructure (i.e. highways, bridges, dams, railroads, etc.)
- Replacing the nation's aging electrical grid
- Updating the national air traffic control system
- Requiring more specific and accurate labelling of food as well as improving the safety and inspection standards for food
- Adopting a single payer health insurance system
- Overhauling the U.S. nuclear arsenal
- Adopting a system of mental health care treatment
- Increasing inspections at U.S. nuclear plants
- Eliminating funding for all military research and development projects and setting up a panel of DOD experts to have public hearings about what the DOD needs and doesn't need
- Closing most foreign military bases
- Withdrawing from the NATO military alliance
- Fixing and privatizing (selling) AMTRAK to provide high-speed passenger service to every major city in America

I'm sure that one of the questions that many people would have is how would you guarantee that these elected officials would go to Congress and do what the supporters want them to do. Well, that brings us to the next step in the process of organizing the reform movement. Through the website, the supporters of the movement would be required to identify people in their community that they know would be ideal candidates for Congress. This is where the onus would be on all of us in identifying trustworthy, noble, and intelligent people for Congress. More importantly, we would want to identify people who have never held political office and have never sought political office. Why? Well, people who have held or sought political office are typically ambitious. Guess what? The people we currently have serving in the U.S. Congress are ambitious and look where that's gotten us as a nation. So as I said, we would want to identify trustworthy, noble, and intelligent people for Congress who have no designs on political office. We all know people that we respect, admire, and believe to be intelligent. If we could convince these people to seek office by essentially drafting them for office. This process guarantees that the folks we put forward as candidates would be the best among us and much more likely to carry out the mission of the reform movement by actually introducing the reform movement's bills and advocating for their passage in Congress against the Democratic and Republican parties.

There will need to be 435 individuals nominated for each of the U.S. House's 435 congressional districts across America in addition to the 100 U.S. Senators. Now, there will be thousands of persons identified but once the deadline for identifying the best and brightest among us for office has passed, the sixty million supporters of the reform movement would vote online for nominees to represent the movement in each of the 435 congressional districts and each of the 100 senate seats for the upcoming general election. As for the onerous signature requirements that most states impose on third party and independent candidates getting their names on the ballot, the movement will have organizers in each congressional district that will be responsible for securing the signatures from among the movement's supporters to secure the ballot access needed in each of the states (as the requirements differ from state to state).

The long term goal for the reform movement would be to obtain a veto proof majority in both houses of Congress so that the movement wouldn't have to rely on whoever the president is at the time to sign its bills into law. If the Democratic or Republican president vetoes a bill passed by the Congress, with a vote of two-thirds of both houses the bill would still become law. It may take three or four general elections to acquire the majority needed (because of the structural impediments in the election of senators) to carry forward the legislative agenda of the reform movement but perseverance will get it done.

The final piece needed to complete the reform movement is raising money. Currently, it takes about $1.5 million for a single candidate to get elected to the U.S .House of Representatives and about $8.5 million for a senate candidate to get elected to the U.S. Senate. What that means is that it would take about $652.5 million to run candidates for all 435 House seats and about $850 million to run candidates for all 100 Senate seats. That adds up to about $1.5 billion. However, this movement wouldn't need that much money. As long as there are sixty to eighty million Americans who support the reform movement there wouldn't be a need to raise as much money to do the typical things that politicians use the money to do.

Remember, political candidates that have little or no name recognition spend millions of dollars to tell the voters who they are. This is largely done in television advertisements. In addition to telling the voters who they are, political candidates also try to negatively define their opponents. Television ad costs are extremely expensive. However, the reform movement wouldn't need as much money. First, the movement would have the support of sixty to eighty million Americans, which would be guaranteed votes in each of the congressional districts and states because of these people's desire to change and save their country as previously mentioned. Secondly, the movement would be able to raise up to $300 million by asking for $5 from each of its sixty million supporters. This money would we used to run political ads to reach Americans who hadn't already joined the reform effort by explaining what the movement is trying to achieve and to support its political candidates.

Now, Americans have a famous reputation for having short attention spans. The only way any major reform movement can be successful is for its public supporters to remain steadfast and not become disillusioned because one election doesn't result in instant change. Remember, it will take some time to take control of the U.S. Senate because of its staggered elections.

Another use for those veto proof majorities (two-thirds) would be to allow the reform movement to advance any proposed constitutional amendments that it wants and send them to state ratifying conventions instead of state legislatures. The U.S. Constitution allows for proposed constitutional amendments to be considered for ratification by either the state legislature or state ratifying conventions. Using state ratifying conventions, as opposed to state legislatures, to let Americans directly decide whether to amend the Constitution thereby rendering the state-based Democratic and Republican parties' control of state legislatures void. The two parties wouldn't be able to kill the proposed constitutional amendments through legislative maneuvers. Instead, the voters of the fifty states would elect delegates to state ratifying conventions where they would decide whether to ratify (i.e. affirm) the proposed amendments. If 38 state ratifying conventions affirm the proposed amendments, they become part of the Constitution.

Now this entire plan of action or plan for reform, whatever you choose to call it, makes it sound like an easy lift. Of course it's not an easy lift. This would be one of the heaviest lifts for the American people to achieve but it's our last stand for our liberty and our democracy. It would require a core group of dedicated citizens of several hundred thousand to keep the sixty to eighty million supporters of the movement engaged over the period of six to eight years that it would take to solidify control over the entirety of the Congress.

Even if the reform movement isn't able to obtain its veto proof super majority or simple majority in either house of Congress, the reform movement may be able to get a substantial number of House and Senate seats, which would give the movement power. The power to form a coalition with either party that would be willing to advance the people's legislative agenda as established by the vote on the reform movement's website. In the alternative and if neither party wanted to work with the reform movement's senators and representatives, they could still introduce the people's bills on the floor of Congress and, when they are defeated in floor votes or not allowed to come to the floor for votes, the people would have more justification to remove the Democrats and Republicans who stand in the way at the next general election. The point of all of this is that perseverance is the key to the success of any reform effort. One election would not result in the change we need.

This reform movement would require a coalition of progressives, liberals, and libertarians to disavow their allegiance to the Democratic and Republican parties if they truly want to change their country. They would have to give up their single issue causes like guns, gay marriage, genetically modified organisms, or other important, but ancillary, issues in the face of the crisis we face with this current government. Together we would be able to eliminate the corporate influence over our government, re-establish the importance of individual liberty in this society, and make this country function as a republic should.

BIBLIOGRAPHY

Books & Reports

Escalasco, Mark, <u>Chile Under Pinochet: Recovering the Truth</u>, (Philadelphia: University of Pennsylvania Press, 2000).

Freeman, Joanne B., <u>Writings: Alexander Hamilton</u>, (New York: The Library of America, Literary Classics of the United States, Inc., 2001).

Gaustad, Edwin S., <u>Roger Williams: Prophet of Liberty</u> (New York: Oxford University Press, Inc., 2001).

Kean, Thomas & Lee Hamilton, <u>The 9/11 Commission Report</u>, National Commission on Terrorist Attacks Upon the United States.

King Jr., Martin Luther, *Letter From Birmingham Jail*, <u>Why We Can't Wait</u>, (City: Mentor of the Penguin Group, 1964).

Laqueur, Walter, <u>Fascism: Past, Present, Future</u> (New York: Oxford University Press, Inc., 1996).

Lemay, J.A. Leo editor, <u>Franklin: Essays, Articles, Bagatelles, and Letters, Poor Richard's Almanack, Autobiography</u>, (New York: The Library of America, Literary Classics of the United States, Inc., 1987).

Locke, John, <u>Two Treatises on Government</u>.

Marty, Dick, <u>Secret Detentions and Illegal transfers of detainees involving Council of Europe member states: second report</u>, Committee on Legal Affairs and Human Rights, June 7, 2007.

Rakove, Jack N. editor, <u>James Madison, Writings</u> (New York: The Library of America, Literary Classics of the United States, Inc., 1999).

Wills, Gary Editor, <u>The Federalist Papers by Alexander Hamilton, James Madison, and John Jay</u>, (New York: Bantam Books, 1982).

President George W. Bush, <u>Address to a Joint Session of Congress and the American People</u>, September 20, 2001.

Court Cases

<u>Gratz v. Bollinger</u>, 539 U.S. 244 (2003).
<u>Grutter v. Bollinger</u>, 539 U.S. 306 (2003).

Hamdan v. Rumsfeld, 548 U.S. 557 (2006)

Mayfield et al. v. USA, 04-1427-AA

Roper v. Simmons, 543 U.S. 551 (2005)

U.S.A. v. Paradise, 480 U.S. 149 (1987).

U.S.A. v. Ressam, Chief Judge John Coughenour, U.S. v. Ressam Transcript, July 27, 2005.

News Articles

Bush Administration on Iraq 9/11 link BBC http://news.bbc.co.uk/go/pr/fr/-/2/hi/americas/3119676.stm. Published September 18, 2003.

Bush rejects Saddam 9/11 link http://news.bbc.co.uk/go/pr/fr/-/2/hi/americas/3118262.stm. Published September 18, 2003.

CNN's Reliable Sources, Are Journalists Jumping on the Bush Bandwagon, Aired October 6, 2001, http://www.cnn.com/transcripts.

Eric Schmitt, "House Panel Backs B-2 But No More Seawolf Subs," *New York Times*, May 24, 1995.

Jan Sliva, "Probe of CIA Prisons Implicates EU Nations," *Tacoma News Tribune (Associated Press)*, June 7, 2006.

Vick, Karl and David Finkel, "Activists in Iran say U.S. strategy hurts their work," *The Seattle Times (Washington Post)*, March 14, 2006.

"40 years for white supremacist," *The Seattle Times (Associated Press)*, April 7, 2005.

Warren Richey, "Analysts split in assessing courts' role in Schiavo case," *The Seattle Times (The Christian Science Monitor)*, April 4, 2005.

Peter Wallstein, "Evangelical groups seek "defunding" of judges," *The Seattle Times (Los Angeles Times)*, April 23, 2005.

CNN's Reliable Sources, Are Journalists Jumping on the Bush Bandwagon, Aired October 6, 2001, http://www.cnn.com/transcripts.

Josh Meyer, "Officials poke holes in Bush's case for wiretaps," *The Seattle Times (Los Angeles Times)*, December 22, 2005, http://www.seattletimes.com.

Craig, Tim and Michael D. Shear, "Senator says he's sorry for "macaca" comment," *Seattle Times (Washington Post)*, August 15, 2006.

Steven Thomma, "Senator Links Gift To Bank Of China -- Specter: $50,000 Came To Democrats," *Knight-Ridder Newspapers*, July 11, 1997.

The NewsHour with Jim Lehrer Transcript, The Public Broadcasting Station, September 14, 1998, http://www.pbs.org/newshour/bb/remember/july-dec98/wallace_9-14.html.

Federal Intervention in Schiavo Case Prompts Broad Public Disapproval, copyright 2005, http://abcnews.com/pollvault.html.

The Terri Schiavo Case: The Paradoxically Most U.S. Adults Approve of How Both Her Husband and Her Parents Behaved, Harris Interactive Inc. Copyright 2005, http://www.harrisinteractive.com/harris_poll/index.asp?PID=558

INDEX

Abraham Lincoln, **95, 172, 184**

Adolf Hitler, **19, 89, 138**

African Americans, **2, 6, 87, 88, 162, 166, 167, 168, 172, 173, 175, 176, 182, 183, 185, 186, 188, 189, 190, 191, 192, 193, 194, 197, 198, 199, 200**

Ahmed Ressam, **114, 118**

Al Jazeera, **91, 159**

Al Qaeda, **21, 26, 31, 32, 33, 34, 93, 101, 103, 106, 107, 109, 115, 117, 118, 123, 124, 127, 159, 186, 187, 203**

Alberto Gonzalez, **113**

Al-Jazeera, **100, 101, 102**

Andrew Johnson, **156**

Anti-Federalists, **54, 71, 72, 74, 75, 80**

Attorney General John Ashcroft, **32, 125**

Augusto Pinochet, **149, 151, 152**

Bill of Rights, **8, 55, 57, 71, 73, 74, 75, 80, 94, 95, 218, 231, 234**

Blackwater, **50**

Brownshirts, **36, 91**

Bush Administration, **21, 26, 27, 31, 32, 33, 34, 35, 37, 40, 50, 85, 86, 89, 90, 93, 96, 98, 99, 101, 104, 113, 115, 116, 118, 119, 124, 125, 147, 158, 203, 238, 244, 245, 260**

Central Intelligence Agency, **91**

Christianity, **15, 51, 52, 58, 59, 64, 65, 69, 73, 75, 78**

civil liberties, **26, 54, 55, 83, 84, 85, 89, 97, 103, 107, 114, 117, 121, 147, 152, 235**

Civil Rights, **4, 23, 168, 169, 173, 174, 183, 187, 200**

classical conservatism, **12, 13**

Condoleezza Rice, **92**

Conservatives, **v, 6, 17, 20, 35, 48, 52, 55, 63, 64, 74, 81, 85, 94, 99, 110, 123, 124, 165, 170, 178, 189, 193, 199, 202, 203, 205, 206, 207, 209, 216, 220, 224, 229, 230, 237**

Constitutional Convention, **8, 75, 170**

Corporatism, **18**

Creationism

  Intelligent Design, 58, 59

Declaration of Independence, 43

democratic, 10, 57, 58, 103, 129, 130, 131, 132, 145, 147, 148, 153, 164, 230, 246

Dixiecrat, 173, 180

Dwight D. Eisenhower, 40, 141

Economic imperialism, 48

Establishment Clause, 73, 74

Fascist, 22, 42

Federal Bureau of Investigations

  FBI, 32

Federalists, 54, 71, 73, 75, 76, 79, 80

First Amendment, 32, 36, 74, 79, 88, 91, 93, 219, 231, 233

FISA, 104, 106, 111, 112, 113

Foreign Intelligence Surveillance Act

  FISA, 104

Founding Fathers, 9, 10, 11, 13, 55, 57, 58, 64, 65, 71, 73, 74, 77, 79, 80, 84, 94, 110, 146,

228, 234

Framers, 135, 208, 210, 211, 212, 213, 214, 217, 219, 220, 222, 231, 232, 233, 235, 247

Franklin D. Roosevelt, 95

Free Exercise Clause, 73, 74

French Revolution, 13, 14, 15

George C. Wallace, 198

Germans, 19, 26, 53

Guantanamo Bay Naval Base, 90, 109

Gulf of Tonkin incident, 38

Halliburton, 50

Harry Truman, 96, 173

Henry Kissinger, 134, 150

Hurricane Katrina, 1, 50, 245

Imperialism, 18, 42

Iraq War, 21, 35, 37

Islam, 59, 63, 106, 138

James Madison, 71, 72, 73, 75, 77, 80, 84, 94, 121, 219, 231, 232, 234, 259

Jerry Falwell, 62, 204

Jesse Helms, 23, 154, 168, 177

Jessica Lynch, 37, 38

Jim Crow, 5, 88, 166, 167, 168, 169, 172, 175, 177, 181, 186, 189, 191, 193, 197, 199

John Coughenour, 115, 116, 260

Kemal Ataturk, 146

liberal, 1, 4, 7, 9, 15, 17, 24, 33, 37, 53, 57, 58, 61, 100, 103, 123, 132, 142, 145, 153, 159, 160, 164, 180, 233, 239, 241, 242, 244

liberals, 5, 8, 61, 62, 94, 123, 188, 230, 237, 246, 256

Marshall Plan, 135, 136, 162, 164

Massachusetts Bay Colony, 67, 76

Michael Moore, 36, 93

Militarism, 18

Mohammad Reza, 138, 139, 145

Mohammed Mossadegh, 139

Muslims, 123, 124, 127, 128

National Security Agency, 90, 111, 250

Nationalism, 18, 25

Native American, 43, 52, 69, 87

Nazi, 19, 20, 89, 91, 138, 161, 169, 183

Palestinian, 128, 130, 161, 162

Pat Robertson, 53, 62, 204

plural, 9, 57, 58, 86, 103, 132, 145, 153, 164

Plymouth Colony, 68

President Franklin Delano Roosevelt, 48, 209, 240

President George W. Bush, 2, 21, 36, 99, 115, 158, 159, 180, 229, 259

Racism, 18

Religion, 18, 69, 77

republic, 4, 10, 29, 53, 57, 58, 64, 77, 78, 86, 94, 99, 121, 133, 144, 145, 160, 209, 231, 248, 257

Revolutionary War, 44, 55

Richard M. Nixon, 96, 150, 175

Richard Nixon, 150

Roger Williams, 67, 68, 70, 76, 258

Ronald Reagan, 35, 40, 127, 153, 176, 236

Rudy Giuliani, 47

Rule of Law, 11, 56, 211, 213, 216, 218, 224, 225

Saddam Hussein, 21, 27, 33, 34, 101, 102, 157, 158

Salvador Allende Gossens, 149

Sam Brownback, 178

Sandinistas, 155

Somozas, 154

Stephen Harper, 97

Strom Thurmond, 23, 173, 179, 200

Taliban, 33, 37, 53, 54, 56, 58, 61, 62, 63, 90, 108, 117, 159, 164, 203

U.S.A. PATRIOT Act

Patriot Act, 85

U.S.S. Cole, 113, 127

United Kingdom, 36, 66, 97, 119, 136, 138, 140, 145, 162, 248

USA PATRIOT Act, 104

Valerie Plame, 89

Vice President Dick Cheney, 92

Winston Churchill, 141

World Trade Center, 26, 34, 103, 104, 127, 199

ABOUT THE AUTHOR

Charles has an extensive amount of experience in the machinations of government after nine years of managing claims and litigation against the State of Washington in addition to the knowledge he acquired while earning his B.A. in political science from Western Washington University and J.D. from Willamette University College of Law. Charles also serves as a professional mediator assisting disputing parties in settling their legal issues as well as teaches two introductory legal courses at Pierce College.

Charles resides in the beautiful Puget Sound region with his wonderful wife and two amazing children. In his spare, time Charles writes fiction as well. His first published title is *The Rise of Annie Lone*, which is available on Amazon in paperback and e-book format as well as in e-book form at Barnes and Noble and Kobo.